THE DAYBOOK OF
S·A·I·N·T·S

THE DAYBOOK OF
S·A·I·N·T·S

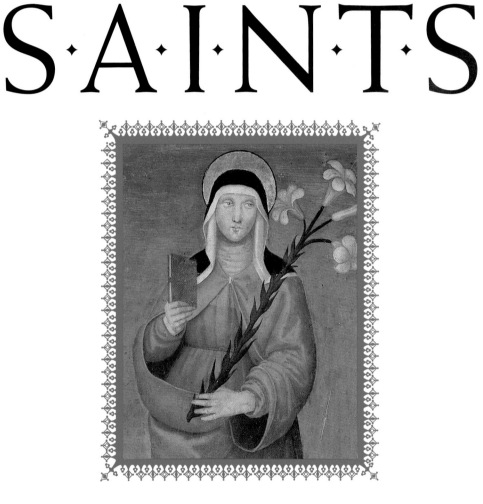

A CELEBRATION OF SAINTS THROUGHOUT THE YEAR

TERRY MATZ

Viking Studio
Published by the Penguin Group
Penguin Putnam Inc., 375 Hudson Street
New York, New York 10014, U.S.A.
Penguin Books Ltd, 27 Wrights Lane,
London W8 5TZ, England
Penguin Books Australia Ltd, Ringwood,
Victoria, Australia
Penguin Books Canada Ltd, 10 Alcorn Avenue,
Toronto, Ontario, Canada M4V 3B2
Penguin Books (N.Z.) Ltd, 182-190 Wairau Road,
Auckland 10, New Zealand

Penguin Books Ltd, Registered Offices:
Harmondsworth, Middlesex, England

First American edition
Published in 2001 by Viking Studio,
a member of Penguin Putnam Inc.

10 9 8 7 6 5 4 3 2 1

Copyright © Mitchell Beazley 2000
All rights reserved

CIP data available
ISBN 0-670-89452-4

Printed in China
by Toppan Printing Company Ltd
Typeset in Weiss
Designed by Christine Keilty

PAGE 1 *St Nicholas, Bishop of Myra.*

PAGE 2 *St Francis of Assisi, and his mystical marriage.*

PAGE 3 *St Clare of Assisi.*

C O N T E N T S

Saints are featured on each day of the month.

INTRODUCTION

 MORE THAN PLASTER STATUES When you mention the word "saint," many picture someone with their eyes perpetually rolled up to heaven, who never laughs or indulges in fun pastimes, who has always led a perfect life, who never makes a mistake – in other words, a plaster religious statue rather than someone who is more like you or me.

In reality, saints represent the whole spectrum of human experience. In this book you will find saints who were queens and saints who were slaves; saints who founded universities as well as educational failures. There were saints who were contemplative hermits and saints who were gregarious world travellers; some were millionaires and others were beggars. Some saints lived past 100 years of age but others were martyred by the

age of 12 – they all appear alongside saints who had happy marriages and successful careers as well as those who struggled with anger, fear, depression, addiction, disabilities, and abuse. Other saints clowned around, loved to make people laugh, and were impulsive and impetuous. Some saints also formed deep friendships, and loved intensely. You will find saints of all these types and everything in between. In other words, you will find saints who were ordinary people working at everyday tasks.

So who is a saint? A saint is someone who was committed to a life of holiness, centred on God, lived out in whatever circumstances or struggles he or she faced. Saints are recognized for having shown heroic virtue in the ways they lived and died.

NAMING SAINTS Although all religions have models of holiness, the Roman Catholic Church is the only religious institution with a formal process for naming new saints. The Catholic Church doesn't make people saints but rather beatification and canonization recognize what God's grace has already accomplished.

In 1983, Pope John Paul II simplified and streamlined the canonization process for saints. For a person's "cause" to be considered, the "Servant of God" (as the person is referred to) must be dead, usually for at least five years. Although many might be able to think of people who are living that they feel deserve the name "saint," one of the criteria for canonization by the Catholic Church is evidence that the Servant of God is in heaven with Him. Since saints are so named because of their value to the whole church, evidence showing that ordinary people venerate the person as holy is also needed. The local bishop of the diocese in which the saint lived can then initiate an investigation into the person's life to determine if he or she lived a life of heroic virtue and/or died as a martyr for the faith. The Servant of God's writings, personal or public, are also investigated for orthodoxy of doctrine. Once the bishop determines that there is a potential for canonization, the saint's cause is submitted to panels of theologians at the Vatican, bishops and cardinals, and ultimately the pope who, if he approves, will declare the Servant of God "venerable," or worthy of veneration for holiness.

Beatification proclaims the Servant of God blessed, and occurs if it is determined that they died as a martyr for the faith or, alternatively, if there is proof of one miracle that occurred through their intercession. This miracle must have taken place after the person's death, as evidence that they are in heaven. Reported miracles are examined by doctors and theologians who must determine that there is no medical or other physical explanation for the event. Once beatified, the person can then be added to local or particular church calendars and held up as a model of holiness. One more miracle is required for the beatified person to be canonized and named in the canon (list) of saints worthy of universal veneration.

LEFT *Sts Philip, James, and Bartholomew.* ABOVE *Sts Margaret and Faith.*

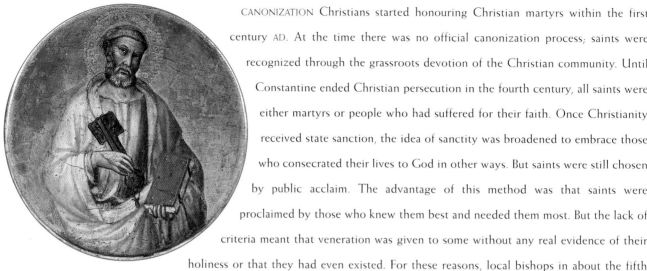

CANONIZATION Christians started honouring Christian martyrs within the first century AD. At the time there was no official canonization process; saints were recognized through the grassroots devotion of the Christian community. Until Constantine ended Christian persecution in the fourth century, all saints were either martyrs or people who had suffered for their faith. Once Christianity received state sanction, the idea of sanctity was broadened to embrace those who consecrated their lives to God in other ways. But saints were still chosen by public acclaim. The advantage of this method was that saints were proclaimed by those who knew them best and needed them most. But the lack of criteria meant that veneration was given to some without any real evidence of their holiness or that they had even existed. For these reasons, local bishops in about the fifth century decided that any new saints had to be approved by them before being added to the calendar. By 1170, Pope Alexander III declared that no new saint could be venerated as a saint without papal approval. Canonization continued to develop over the next few centuries until codified by Benedict XIV in the 18th century. This process affected new saints only – saints who had been venerated for hundreds of years were not re-examined; they simply retained their status. Although the canonization process guaranteed that each new saint would be examined thoroughly, it was such an expensive and adversarial process that only a few hundred saints were canonized over the next 300 years.

Local dioceses and religious orders had always had their own calendars of feast days. The first universal church calendar that organized these separate and often conflicting calendars into one list wasn't published until the 17th century. Then, in 1969, the Catholic Church issued a reformed calendar. The saints on the old calendars were examined once again for any historical evidence of their holiness and for their relevance to the universal church. The new calendar was then put together, based on the findings of this research. This calendar was in fact missing some popular saints, such as Catherine of Alexandria, because there was no evidence that they had existed or lived a holy life.

ABOVE *The Apostle Peter.* RIGHT *St Catherine of Siena.*

One goal of the calendar reform was to create a universal calendar that reflected the universal church. Saints on this universal calendar, whose feast days would be celebrated throughout the church, would be relevant to the church as a whole, as well as represent the multicultural nature of the church. For that reason, some saints were moved from the universal calendar to local calendars but this was not without controversy. St Christopher, for example, was moved to local calendars because there was little evidence that he actually existed. However, his veneration dates from ancient times so his cult was not completely suppressed but confined to local devotion.

CONFLICTING FEAST DAYS AND VARYING SAINTS' NAMES The feast day often coincides with the date of a saint's death because, since the beginning of the church, this has been considered the day on which the saint was reborn and entered their eternal life in heaven. Other feast days are chosen to mark the day when the saint's body (referred to as "relics") was transferred to a cathedral or church, signifying the veneration the saint had received. But feast days may be moved or changed for a variety of reasons. For example, Albert Chmielowski (June 17), actually died close to Christmas, but because of the priority of the Christmas season and other celebrations during that time, his feast is celebrated elsewhere on the calendar. A feast day might be moved locally for the same reasons. For example, Jane de Chantal's feast day is generally December 12, but in the Americas this is the feast of Our Lady of Guadalupe, so Jane's feast day was moved to August in the US. There may also be other reasons why a feast day varies from calendar to calendar; such as one area celebrating the date of the saint's death, while another celebrates the translation of their relics. Additionally, many important dates in the lives of saints are conflicting

because accurate records of births and deaths were often lost. In these instances, we have chosen the most probable dates for the lifespan, though other sources may differ. Where information is conflicting, we have chosen the date that seems the most reliable or the date of the saint's death.

The form of saints' names can vary even more than their feast days. A saint's name can be shown in his or her native language (for example, Giovanni in Italian), be anglicized (to John), or latinized. A saint might be known by a popular name denoting the location of their birth or ministry (Therese of Lisieux), by a religious name if appropriate (Therese of the Child Jesus), or by their family name (Therese Martin). We have chosen and used consistently what we consider to be the most universally recognized form of each saint's name.

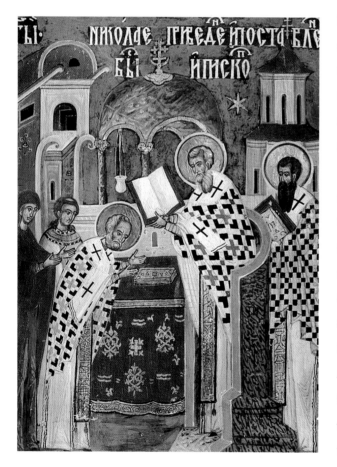

INTERCESSORS AND ROLE MODELS Although we must consider the difference between the saint's culture and time and our own, their virtuous responses to life's challenges can help us to frame our own answers about how to live and serve God. In their mistakes (and yes, even saints made mistakes), we can learn how to transcend our shortcomings by God's grace.

Just as we would ask a friend or loved one to pray for us, many Catholics request the intercession of saints with God. Catholics believe the intimacy saints shared with God during their life continues after their death, making their prayers particularly powerful and effective. Non-Catholics might compare this practice to asking a friend to pray for them in times of need. In this case, Catholics or others who ask for a saint's intercession are requesting that a friend in heaven pray for them. All can appreciate and learn from these holy men and women of God who have become role models through their sainthood, showing us the way to holiness and intimacy with God through their exemplary lives.

The Catholic Church also believes in the communion of saints. This means that the mystical body of Christ that is the church does not just include the members on earth, but all the souls who have gone before us and now watch over us, caring about what happens to us. Because of this communion, we can always feel as if we have unseen but very real companions in our faith journey.

LIVING SAINTS Many holy people throughout the centuries have lived and died in God's grace but have not become part of an official church calendar. You may know people in your own life who have taught you how to be generous, compassionate, or devout, though their virtue remains hidden from the world at large. As Christians we are all called to holiness – Jesus calls us to be perfect as our Father in heaven is perfect (Mt 5:48) and St Paul tells us that God wants more than our salvation, He wants our glorification (Rom 8:30). God wants not only to save us but to transform our lives and use us to accomplish His purposes in the world. The parent, manager, person with disabilities – each one of us – can find examples in this book of people who shared our station and situation in life and fulfilled that destiny. No one has an excuse to say, "A saint? Not someone like me," because somewhere out there a saint's life says, "Yes. Exactly like you."

A FINAL NOTE The following saints were chosen for this book to reflect the variety of cultures and experiences of the people of God. In the spirit of ecumenism, many saints of the Orthodox and Eastern rite Churches are included as they are often venerated in Roman Catholic devotion. All are celebrated by the church as saints, by popular acclaim before the canonization process was formalized, or through official recognition by the church since then via beatification or canonization. Each saint's entry in this book shows a name by which they are commonly known, a "title" summing up their occupation or role within the church, and the most widely accepted dates of their birth and death. A list of other saints sharing the feast day follow each featured saint and an index at the back will help you to locate the saints by name.

Joan of Arc had visions revealing that God had chosen her to save France.

1

ZDISLAVA BERKA
Wife and mother b.1200, d.1252

Zdislava spent her life trying to create a sanctuary of peace for herself and others in her native Bohemia (now part of the Czech Republic). Her arranged marriage to the Count of Lemberk produced four children but his worldly perspective clashed with her spiritual one. He had no sympathy for her prayer life or work with the poor. Despite his opposition, she opened their castle to refugees fleeing the Tartar invasions. Her husband was eventually won over by her patience and by a vision that revealed a beggar she had sheltered to be Christ. Later, she found her spiritual home as a lay member of a Dominican order and built a Dominican convent – literally, since she not only funded the construction but also carried heavy beams to the building site.

OTHER SAINTS • ODILO • JOSEPH TOMASI

2

BASIL THE GREAT &
GREGORY NAZIANZEN
Bishops and Doctors of the Church b.329, d.379/b.329, d.390

When these two men first met as students in Athens, they discovered they were "one soul that had two bodies" as Gregory put it. They withdrew to a wilderness monastery to live in prayer and solitude. Their friendship continued when Basil was forced into public life. Basil then encouraged the humble Gregory to accept ordination as a priest. And Gregory helped Basil endure an archbishop that was jealous of Basil's work. Basil himself became archbishop and worked for social justice, publishing definitive works on the Holy Spirit and the Trinity before his death in 379. Gregory was appointed bishop of Constantinople in 378, but heretic mobs forced him to retire. He spent his life praying and writing until he joined his friend Basil forever.

OTHER SAINTS • SERAPHIM OF SAROV • GASPARE DEL BUFALO

*St Cloud being presented before the Virgin and Child
by Sts Genevieve and Clotilde.*

3

GENEVIEVE OF PARIS
Virgin and patroness of Paris b.422, d.500

When Genevieve was seven years old, St Germanus picked her out of a crowd on the outskirts of Paris and encouraged her to dedicate her life to Christ. Her holy life became widely known; when the army of the Franks starved Paris, it was Genevieve who travelled upriver to get food. The conqueror, Childeric, knew he couldn't refuse anything she asked, so he locked her in the city during the time he planned to execute prisoners. She pursued him, however, by opening the gate with a touch, and eventually won the prisoners' pardon from him. When Attila the Hun threatened Paris in 451, Genevieve organized prayer and fasting for their deliverance. Attila turned away, sparing the city, and this won Genevieve an enduring place as the protector of Paris.

4

ELIZABETH BAYLEY SETON
First native-born US saint b.1774, d.1821

Raised in an Anglican family in New York City, Elizabeth lived a happy life as a wife and mother until her husband went bankrupt and then caught tuberculosis. Shattered by his death in a freezing quarantine cell in Italy, where they'd gone to seek a cure, Elizabeth took refuge with Italian friends who were Catholic. Their kindness led Elizabeth to embrace the Catholic faith. Back in America, however, her family and friends rejected her because of her conversion. She had to take on four jobs just to feed her five children. When word of her remarkable teaching ability reached Baltimore, the bishop invited her to open a school there, which became the first of many. In 1809, she established the first religious congregation founded in the US, the Daughters of Charity of St Joseph, to nurse the sick and teach children.

OTHER SAINTS • ROGER OF ELLANT

5

JOHN NEPOCENE NEUMANN
Bishop and Redemptorist priest b.1811, d.1860

John's dream to become a priest seemed hopeless when he learned that no bishop would ordain him because of a surplus of priests in his native Bohemia. Determined to fulfil his vocation, John sailed to America where he'd heard priests were greatly needed, and arrived in Manhattan, New York in June 1836. John Dubois, the bishop of New York, was glad to ordain John and assigned him to a German-speaking parish in the western part of the state, which stretched from Lake Ontario to Pennsylvania. There John lived above a tavern and preached in a church without steeple or floor, climbing mountains to visit the sick and celebrating Mass at kitchen tables. It was a lonely life, however, and his search for community led him to join the Redemptorists, where he was given much more responsibility. While vice-provincial of the Redemptorists in the United States, he became a US citizen in 1847. Later, as superior of St Alphonsus Church in Baltimore, he slept close

> *"...despite financial troubles, he built over 90 churches and was the first bishop to organize a diocesan Catholic school system in the US."*

to the front door so that he could respond immediately to any request. He reluctantly accepted consecration as bishop of Philadelphia in 1852 where he was scorned by the city's elite for being a small, immigrant, country priest. Undeterred, and despite financial troubles, he built over 90 churches and was the first bishop to organize a diocesan Catholic school system in the US, which boasted 80 schools in John's lifetime. Additionally he learned Spanish, French, Italian, Dutch, and Gaelic so that he could minister to the new immigrants. But he never lost his humility. When someone suggested he change his shoes after they had been soaked in the rain, he replied that the only way he could change his shoes was by switching each shoe to a different foot. He only owned one pair. John collapsed on the streets of Philadelphia and was buried in the first new pair of shoes anyone had seen him wear.

OTHER SAINTS • SIMEON STYLITES

6

BLESSED ANDRE BESSETTE
Holy Cross Brother and porter b.1845, d.1937

Alfred Bessette was an unlikely candidate for a teaching order like the Holy Cross Brothers. Though pious in character, he was illiterate and had never kept a job long because of chronic illness. Only a bishop's intervention in 1870 turned Alfred into Brother Andre, and he was assigned as porter to a Montreal boys school. Brother Andre joked that his superiors had shown him the door, and he stayed there for 40 years. In 1904, when he was 60, he began to build a mountain chapel to St Joseph with nickel donations. Over the years he added to the small wooden shrine – first a roof, then walls, then heating. He died when he was 90 years old, after being carried up the mountain to view the construction his devotion had made possible.

OTHER SAINTS • PETER OF CANTERBURY

7

RAYMOND OF PEÑAFORT
Dominican friar and writer b.1175?, d.1275

Raymond gave the church its primary reference work for canon law for more than 600 years. Born in Catalonia, he taught law before being ordained a priest. At 47, he became a Dominican and wrote a book for confessors, the first of its kind. As a result, Pope Gregory IX appointed Raymond his personal confessor and commissioned him to organize and analyze all the papal and conciliar decrees since 1150. It took three years for Raymond to complete the five volumes of the *Decretals* on canon law. As master general of the Dominican Order, he rewrote the constitutions of the Order. He then used his own rule to resign – citing his age of 65 as the reason. The "retired" Raymond then spent the next 34 years back in Spain, promoting an education in theology and languages for priests.

OTHER SAINTS • BRANNOC • KENTIGERNA • LUCIAN

St Raymond rewrote the constitutions of the Dominican Order.

8

GUDULA OF BRUSSELS
Virgin and patroness of Brussels d.712

Gudula learned what it meant to be holy from her mother, St Almaberga, and her cousin, St Gertrude, who educated her at her convent at Nivelles. After Gertrude's death in 664, Gudula returned to her family in Brabant, Belgium, where she lived as a hermit in her own home. Every morning she walked to an oratory two miles from her castle, sometimes barefoot. She was known for her generosity to anyone in need, as well as for her miracles. One day she took a disabled boy off the shoulders of his mother. When she prayed, his limbs straightened. Gudula, embarrassed by what had happened, begged the mother to say nothing. Of course, the mother disobeyed, adding to Gudula's reputation for sanctity, which led her to be revered as patroness of Brussels.

OTHER SAINTS • NATHALAN • PEGA • WULSIN • THORFINN

9

ADRIAN OF CANTERBURY
African abbot d.710

In 665, this African abbot was secure in his position over a monastery near Naples. Then a bishop from the young church in England died in Rome without a successor. Pope St Vitalian thought Adrian's scholarship, discipline, and travel experience made him an ideal candidate for the position. Adrian begged to be relieved of the responsibility and the pope agreed – if Adrian found a substitute and went to Britain as his assistant. In 668, Adrian left Naples forever with the new Archbishop Theodore. After a difficult journey they arrived in England, and he was appointed abbot of Sts Peter and Paul in Canterbury where he taught not just religious subjects but poetry, astronomy, and arithmetic. Yet, true to his word, his first responsibility was in helping Theodore, and he visited local tribes and instructed them in the faith.

OTHER SAINTS • BERHTWALD • FILLAN

10

MARCIAN OF CONSTANTINOPLE
Priest d.476

A member of the imperial family, Marcian gave to the poor even as a child. After being ordained priest he was appointed treasurer of the Church of Santa Sofia, a position he used to construct and restore many churches. On his way to an important church consecration, he saw a poor man clothed in rags. Marcian had no money to give the man and no time to go back, so he gave the man the tunic he wore under his vestments. Though he was afraid people would notice his missing clothing, the whole congregation instead saw a sparkling golden tunic. So convincing was the vision that the patriarch reprimanded him for wearing such a garment. Marcian also worked diligently to find honest occupations for prostitutes, searching them out to help them.

OTHER SAINTS • DERMOT • PAUL THE HERMIT • SAETHRITH

11

THEODOSIUS THE CENOBIARCH
Monk b.423, d.529

Like many from small towns, Theodosius longed to visit places far from his home in Cappadoccia. After travelling to holy places throughout Palestine, he settled in a mountain cave. Because he welcomed any sincere disciple, he soon needed a place to house a community. He travelled to the Dead Sea and back, praying that God would reveal a location for the monastery, only to receive a sign at the cave he'd started from. His monastery was described as a city of saints, and had infirmaries, hospices for travellers, and four churches. The patriarch of Jerusalem placed him in charge of all the men living in community (cenobites), hence the title Cenobiarch, but the Arian emperor banished him for preaching against heresy. After the emperor's death, Theodosius returned home and was eventually buried in his original cave.

—◆— 12 —◆—

MARGUERITE BOURGEOYS

Canadian teacher and sister b. 1620, d. 1700

Marguerite didn't shrink from challenges; she chased after them. When the governor of Montreal went to France to find someone to organize a school for his infant colony, the stories of hardships and dangers in Montreal that frightened other people awakened a call in Marguerite. When she arrived in Ville Marie, as Montreal was called in 1653, she found a tiny village under constant threat of attack by raiders, illness, and starvation. Since most children died young, her first responsibility as schoolmistress was to help Jeanne Mance, who ran the hospital, to ensure that the children lived long enough to become students. She then held her first classes in a stable. When the king sent over untrained orphans as colonists, she taught them how to survive in the New World. On several trips to France, she convinced women to join her new community of teaching sisters. She built her first boarding school in 1673 and, three years later, her first school for Native Americans. She welcomed two young Iroquois women to her community in 1679. Yet

> *"...the stories of hardships and dangers in Montreal that frightened other people awakened a call in Marguerite."*

hardships were great and threats to her work daunting. Her community survived Iroquois attacks and a fire that destroyed the convent. But the worst threat came when the bishop of Montreal decided that her community should be cloistered – completely shut off from the world. Marguerite's sisters lived in small huts in the woods and travelled all over the frontier to reach the Native Americans and colonists. She convinced the bishop that he would lose a valuable resource if he insisted on traditional roles for women. The bishop finally responded by saying that he had no doubt that she would move heaven and earth as she had moved him. The congregation remained an active teaching order, one of the first for women, and her schools numbered over 200 before her death.

OTHER SAINTS • AILRED • BENEDICT BISCOP • SALVIOS

Marguerite Bourgeoys felt called to Canada and its people.

13

HILARY OF POITIERS
Bishop b.315, d.368

Raised as a pagan, Hilary's search for truth led him through all the schools of philosophy. He found what he sought in the clear definition of God in Exodus 3:14, "I AM WHO I AM" and in the incarnation of Jesus. Three years after his baptism in 350, he was elected bishop of Poitiers, France, though he was married with a daughter. When Hilary protested about the persecution of St Athanasius by Arians, the emperor banished him. But exile gave Hilary time to study Arian arguments that Jesus was not divine and to write works refuting them. When Hilary threatened to take his message to the imperial capital of Constantinople, the emperor sent him back to Poitiers. Hilary took the long way back, preaching against the Arians all the way through Greece and Italy.

OTHER SAINTS • KENTIGERN

14

SAVA OF SERBIA
Bishop and monk b.1174?, d.1235

Sava's father Stefan Nemanja won independence for Serbia from the Byzantine Empire but abdicated in 1196 to join his son in a monastic community in Greece. Together they founded the monastery of Khilandari for Serbian monks on Mount Athos, where books that Sava translated into Serbian are still treasured. After his father's death, Sava returned home to settle a dispute between his brothers but stayed when he realized how much his people needed his help. Sava took monks from Khilandari back to educate the Serbians. He convinced the emperor that Serbians were not barbarians and that they should have their own, native bishops. Legends say that he even taught the Serbians how to make windows and plough fields. With all he accomplished for Serbia it is no wonder that he died with a smile on his face.

OTHER SAINTS • FELIX OF NOLA • MACRINA THE ELDER

15

ITA OF LIMERICK
Irish nun and founder b.480?, d.570

This saint, whose name comes from the word iota, meaning thirst for holiness, is second only in popularity to Brigid in Ireland. Her father, an important leader in the tribe of Decii near Drum, County Waterford, arranged a prestigious marriage for her. Because she wished to consecrate her life to God instead, she prayed and fasted for three days until her father agreed to let her follow her calling. She journeyed to the western area of the present county of Limerick to found a small community of men and women at Killeedy. A chieftain offered her a large gift of land to support the convent but Ita would accept only the four acres that she needed to grow vegetables. Like other ascetics, much of her spiritual life was devoted to quiet contemplation and rigorous self-denial. She became so famous for her holiness, wisdom, and the graces God granted her that a pilgrim asked her

"This saint...is second only in popularity to Brigid in Ireland...

She is called the foster mother of Irish saints..."

why God loved her so much. She responded that it was her practice of continual contemplation of the holy mysteries that gave her the graces to heal, prophesy, and talk with angels. Once when she practiced fasting for three or four days at a time, an angel told her that she should have more respect for the health of her body. She is called the foster mother of Irish saints because she ran a school for boys that included many students later known for their holiness, including St Brendan of Clonfert, St Pulcherius (Mochoemog), and St Cummian Fada. St Brendan once asked her what three things God loved the most. She answered, "True faith with a pure heart, a simple life with a thankful spirit, and generosity with love." When he asked what three things God hated most, she responded, "A face that scowls at everyone, a soul that clings to sin, and a heart that trusts too much in the power of money."

OTHER SAINTS • CEOLWULF • EFISIO • MACARIUS

Sava translated many books into Serbian that are still treasured today.

16

HONORATUS OF ARLES

Bishop and monk b.350?, d.429

In 410, no one could understand why an educated nobleman wanted to live on Lérins, a dry, rocky island off the French Riviera. But Honoratus had always done the unexpected. When his father sent his brother to convince him to renounce Christianity, Honoratus converted his brother instead. Honoratus transformed Lérins into a paradise and the beauty of the land reflected Honoratus's attractive nature, which drew disciples from all nations to his monastery. His relative, St Hilary, said he was like a father to all, striving to create a joyful spiritual existence for them that erased painful memories of the world. His monks were like a community of angels at rest. Honoratus left his island to become bishop of Arles in 426 and died three years later.

OTHER SAINTS • FURSEY • HENRY OF COQUET ISLAND • MARCELLUS

17

ANTHONY

Abbot and founder b.251?, d.356

Anthony wasn't looking for peace, but for a place to struggle with his soul. After hearing the Gospel exhorting the rich to give their money to the poor, Anthony got rid of his estate, entrusted his sister to a convent, and left his Egyptian village for a hermit's life of prayer, fasting, and manual labour. He faced temptations so strong that he felt he actually wrestled with the devil. Seeking even more solitude, Anthony sealed himself in a desert cell. When people wanting his advice broke in, Anthony created what has been called the first monastic community. Anthony taught his disciples that perseverance meant not just endurance, but starting each day with as much enthusiasm as if it were the first day of their lives. Fearing his own pride, he spent his last years alone on a mountain.

OTHER SAINTS • MILDGYTH • SULPICIUS

18

DEICOLUS

Hermit d.625

Deicolus followed St Columbanus through Ireland, England, and France, but, finally, was too exhausted to go on. The friends parted, and Deicolus built a hermitage in the Burgundy wilderness. A local chaplain, unhappy about having a hermit in his congregation, barricaded the chapel with thorn bushes to keep him out and the nobleman who owned the chapel had Deicolus beaten. But when the nobleman was sick, Deicolus hurried to help him. After the man was healed through his prayer, his wife gave Deicolus the chapel and land around it. He eventually built the abbey of Lure on land given to him by King Clothaire II. When Columbanus once asked him why he was always smiling, Deicolus responded, "Because no one can separate my God from me."

OTHER SAINTS • PRISCA • ULFRID

19

WULFSTAN OF WORCESTER

Bishop and Benedictine monk b.1008, d.1095

Wulfstan's spirituality gave him the strength not just to survive a time of great change, but to use that change to serve his people. Born in Worcester, he joined the same Benedictine monastery that his father had entered. When he was elected prior he preached every Sunday to the people. It took the pope, the king, and a hermit to convince Wulfstan to accept his election as bishop of Worcester in 1062. When the Normans conquered England, Wulfstan was the only Saxon bishop to retain his position. Wulfstan forged a strong alliance with the new archbishop of Canterbury, Lanfranc, to abolish the English slave trade with the Irish, to promote clerical celibacy, as well as introduce further reforms. Wulfstan died during his daily ceremony of washing the feet of 12 poor men, which symbolized his dedication to service.

OTHER SAINTS • BRANWALADEN • CANUTE • HENRY OF FINLAND

St Anthony experienced many temptations while he was living as a hermit.

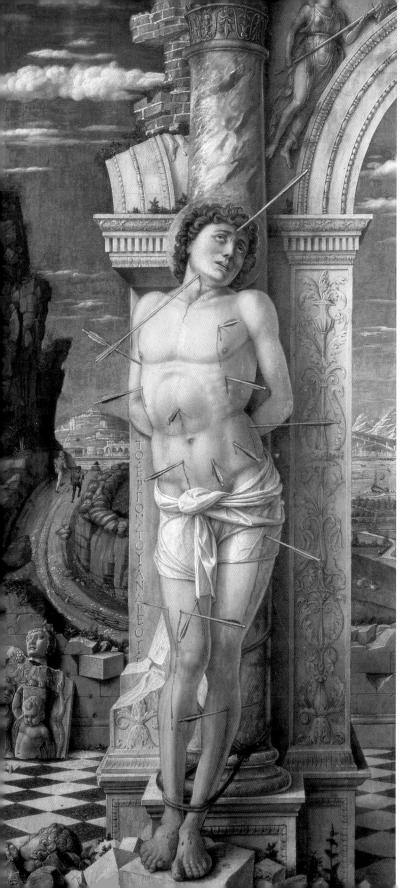

SEBASTIAN
Soldier and martyr d. 288?

Early testimony proclaims that Sebastian died a martyr in Rome, probably in the late third or early fourth century, and was buried in the Appian Way. He was venerated at least as far back as the time of St Ambrose and probably had some connection to Milan. According to later tradition, Sebastian was born in Gaul but raised in Milan. He joined the Roman army during a time of persecution even though he was a Christian. He used his official position to encourage the imprisoned martyrs that he guarded. But the very qualities that he nurtured as a Christian – faithfulness, zealousness, prudence – made him a good soldier, and the Emperor Diocletian promoted him to captain of the Pretorian guards without ever guessing Sebastian's secret. Then, without concern for his own safety, he not only convinced two imprisoned martyrs to remain steadfast but converted the magistrate who had been trying to get them to abandon their faith. Diocletian discovered Sebastian's complicity when the magistrate released the prisoners and took them home with him.

> *"...the very qualities that he nurtured as a Christian – faithfulness, zealousness, prudence – made him a good soldier..."*

The emperor was furious at what he saw as a betrayal of himself and Rome. Sebastian argued that he prayed every day for the prosperity of Rome and the safety of the emperor – he simply prayed to the God of heaven for these blessings. Diocletian was unmoved and ordered Sebastian to be shot by archers. A Christian woman, Irene, found Sebastian still alive and nursed him in her home. When the wounded Sebastian heard the procession of the emperor passing outside, he dragged himself from his sickbed to the window to try to assure him of his loyalty. Sebastian told Diocletian that Christians were not enemies of the state but prayed for the welfare of the empire and their sovereign just like other Romans. Diocletian ignored Sebastian's arguments and had him beaten to death with clubs.

OTHER SAINTS • FABIAN • FECHIN • EUSTOCHIUM • CALATATO

Even after he had ordered archers to shoot Sebastian, the saint remained loyal to Emperor Diocletian.

21

AGNES

Virgin martyr of Rome d. 350?

Both St Ambrose and Pope St Damasus praised this young girl's courage a few decades after her death. According to these saints, Agnes was martyred when she was about 12 during Diocletian's persecution of Christians. Ambrose reports that she was executed by sword after refusing a suitor because she was pledged to Christ, while Damasus says that she was killed in a fire, covered only by her hair. According to later tradition, the governor confined Agnes to a brothel to get her to renounce her faith but she was kept safe through divine protection. When she refused to apostatize, he called her a stubborn child. Agnes replied that faith was not a matter of years but of the heart. When her prayer extinguished her execution pyre, a soldier slit her throat.

OTHER SAINTS • MEINRAD

22

VINCENT OF SARAGOSSA

Deacon and first martyr of Spain d. 304

Young Vincent received instruction in Christianity from the bishop of Saragossa, Spain. Bishop Valerius gave Vincent responsibility for teaching in the diocese after he was ordained deacon. Because Valerius had a speech impediment, Vincent became the bishop's voice and testified for both of them when they were arrested during Diocletian's persecution. Valerius was exiled but Vincent was imprisoned. Augustine described his torture as more than any human could bear without divine help. When the governor offered him a pardon if he gave up Christian books, Vincent responded that he was more afraid of false compassion than torture. Fearing Vincent's power to convert others, the governor finally granted Vincent clemency. But his body was beyond healing; he died with the same peace he had shown during his ordeal.

OTHER SAINTS • BERHTWALD • ANASTASIUS • VINCENT PALLOTI

23

JOHN THE ALMSGIVER

Patriarch of Alexandria b. 552?, d. 616?

John was a wealthy Cypriot widower who gave away all his money to help the poor. When his generosity resulted in his election as patriarch of Alexandria, he asked for a list of his masters – the poor of the city. He not only distributed 80,000 pieces of gold to hospitals and monasteries, but forbade his officers from accepting gifts. He also worked for social reform by regulating the weights used by merchants, to ensure fair pricing. Twice a week, he sat outside the church to listen to the petitions of the poor. His humility was so great that he stopped celebrating Mass once when he remembered Christ's injunction to be reconciled before approaching the altar; he ran to beg forgiveness of a clerk he had excommunicated for a few days.

OTHER SAINTS • EMERENTIANA • ILDEPHONSUS

24

FRANCIS DE SALES

Bishop and founder of the Visitation Order b. 1567, d. 1622

When Francis left France to persuade Calvinists in Switzerland to return to the Catholic Church, he suffered three years of slammed doors, thrown rocks, and freezing winters without seeing anyone converted. Always patient, he worked to win hearts by slipping his sermons under closed doors and playing with children of hostile parents, until he converted 40,000 people. In 1602 he was made bishop of the diocese of Geneva, a Calvinist territory he only saw twice. In 1604 Francis met the widow Jane de Chantal, the dear friend who would lead him to mystical union with God, and together they founded the Visitation Order. With his *Introduction to the Devout Life*, Francis developed something new – a path to holiness for lay people. The book was enormously successful though preachers criticized him for tolerating dancing and jokes!

OTHER SAINTS • BABYLAS • CADOC

—➤ 25 ◆—

PAUL
Apostle of the Gentiles b.4BC?, d.67AD?

This day celebrates the transformation of Saul, the Zealot Jew, to Paul the Apostle of the Gentiles. Saul was born in Tarsus but grew up as a Roman citizen in Jerusalem where he was a disciple of Gamaliel, the most influential rabbi of that time. Paul was a zealous follower of the traditions and laws of the Jewish faith, and was outraged by Christians, whom he perceived as heretic Jews. He went on a campaign to destroy the new sect by any means possible, including violence. He personally approved the stoning of Stephen, who became the first Christian martyr, and dragged Christians out of their homes to prison. So intent was he on stamping Christianity out that he decided to go to Damascus to bring people of the Way, as it was called, back to Jerusalem for punishment. But on his way to Damascus Paul was blinded by an intense light from which he heard the voice of Jesus speaking directly to

"..when Paul preached the gospel that had made Christ live in him, people listened and believed."

him. After this amazing confrontation, he went on to serve Jesus faithfully, under his Latin name of Paul, though he had some trouble convincing the former victims of his persecution of the sincerity of his conversion. When his message was rejected by his fellow Jews, Paul took his good news to the Gentiles (non-Jews), enduring prison, shipwrecks, threats to his life, and other trials on his missionary journeys throughout the Roman empire. Paul then appeared before the Christian elders in Jerusalem to argue that Gentiles should be admitted to the Church without having to follow Jewish law. By his own admission, Paul was not a great preacher. Scripture tells the story of a boy who fell asleep during one of his sermons and fell out of a window. But when Paul preached the Gospel that had made Christ live in him, people listened and believed. Tradition reports that he was beheaded outside Rome during the reign of Nero.

OTHER SAINTS • DWYN • PRAEJECTUS

—➤ 26 ◆—

TIMOTHY AND TITUS
Bishops and disciples of Paul First century

Scriptures tells us that Timothy and Titus were companions of Paul who helped him in his ministry and comforted him in his sufferings. Timothy learned his faith from a Jewish mother and grandmother who were Christian converts. Paul says that Timothy served him like a son in the work of the Gospel, travelling with him as well as visiting young churches. Timothy was killed for his faith in Ephesus. Titus was a Greek Gentile who acted officially as Paul's secretary and interpreter but was also his comforter during times of persecution. According to Paul, Titus accepted assignments with enthusiasm. Paul described Titus as his partner and child in Christ. Titus is recognized as bishop of his native Crete, which is where he died peacefully at an old age.

OTHER SAINTS • ALBERIC • BATHILD • MARGARET OF HUNGARY

—➤ 27 ◆—

ANGELA MERICI
Franciscan tertiary and founder of the Ursuline nuns b.1474, d.1540

In Angela's time, women only received an education if they were wealthy or became nuns. Women weren't allowed to be teachers and unmarried women were prohibited from travelling the streets alone. But Angela was so disturbed by the fate awaiting uneducated poor girls in Lombardy that she broke the rules. Her group of unmarried women, including lay members of the third Order of St Francis, taught girls they gathered from the streets. Angela was so successful that she was invited to take her innovative approach to education to other cities. By the time she was 60, Angela had organized a community of women that grew into the Ursulines, the first group of sisters working outside the cloister and the first teaching order. Angela's radical ideas are now commonplace thanks to her determination to serve others despite criticism.

OTHER SAINTS • DEVOTA • JULIAN OF LE MANS

The spectacular conversion experience of Paul.

28

THOMAS AQUINAS
Dominican friar and theologian b. 1225?, d. 1274

The Dominican friar known to the church as the "Seraphic Doctor" was called a "dumb Sicilian ox" by his classmates in Paris, who mistook his silence for stupidity. His professor, St Albert the Great, discovered Thomas's true intelligence and predicted that the "bellow of this ox would be heard over the whole earth." Through his career in teaching and leading his order, Thomas constructed a system of Christian philosophy using the Greek philosopher Aristotle's deductive science. Thomas's method, known now as scholastic theology, was a radical step in his time, because Aristotle's pagan works had previously been banned. Thomas never finished his *Summa Theologica*, because of a vision that made him realize the divine mystery was beyond his words.

OTHER SAINTS • JOHN THE SAGE • PETER NOLASCO

29

GILDAS THE WISE
Abbot and hermit b. 500?, d. 570?

Gildas influenced monastic life in Wales and Ireland, and also produced a contemporary, if negative, record of British rulers and clergy. Born near Clyde in Scotland, he was educated by saints in the Welsh monastery of Llan Iltut. Gildas was married and St Aidan was one of his many children. He founded several monasteries in Wales and Brittany, including Ile aux Moines. After he accompanied St Patrick to Ireland, Irish monks (who were later famous) became his disciples. In 544, he wrote *De Excidio Britanniae*, blaming the Anglo-Saxon victory on British decadence. This prophetic work, meant to inspire the people to reform their lives, was so inflammatory that his sons and other relatives were forced to leave the country. Gildas himself actually spent his last years as a hermit in Brittany.

OTHER SAINTS • JULIAN THE HOSPITALLER

30

HYACINTHA MARISCOTTI
Franciscan nun and spiritual director b. 1588, d. 1640

Hyacintha Mariscotti, a frivolous young noblewoman, was humiliated when her younger sister married the object of her infatuation. Hyacintha did not handle rejection graciously so her exasperated family pressured her to enter a Franciscan convent. As a student she had been expelled from that convent because she refused to obey the rules. This time, she lived luxuriously in a suite and kept servants. Then a mystical experience of Jesus, revealing the brambles of worldly desires that choked her soul, redirected her life. She exchanged her silk habit for ragged clothes, organized a hospital for the elderly, and set up a charitable relief association. Her gift of discernment made her a popular spiritual director.

31

JOHN BOSCO
Priest and founder of the Salesians b. 1815, d. 1888

The founder of the Salesians had a childhood dream that he was put in charge of a gang of unruly boys. His family laughed at the dream but he never forgot it. He was so poor that his clothes for seminary were provided by neighbours' charity. After he was ordained in 1841, he dedicated himself to teaching poor and neglected boys, whom he attracted with juggling, acrobatics, and tolerance. He succeeded in his mission despite hostile neighbours, who objected to living near hundreds of rowdy street kids, and well-meaning friends who tried to commit him to an insane asylum for pursuing his vision without funding. Some of his students who had vocations to the priesthood became the nucleus of his Salesian Order. When he died, his crazy dream had become an Order with 768 members and schools all over the world.

OTHER SAINTS • MAEDOC OF FERNS

The apotheosis of St Thomas Aquinas.

1

BRIGID OF KILDARE
Abbess and preacher b.455?, d.525?

As a young girl, Brigid so exasperated her family with her generosity that they were probably relieved when she consecrated her life to God at the age of 14. Seeking solitude, she built a hermitage under a large oak tree but her reputation for holiness and talent for leadership soon attracted disciples. The new community was named Kil-dare, or the "Cell of the Oak." Under her direction, Kil-dare grew into the largest town in Ireland, so famous for Brigid's hospitality that it was called the "City of the Poor." Brigid ruled over both nuns and the monks that settled there. Whether or not the stories that she was consecrated bishop are true, her leadership was recognized so widely that she preached around the country and spoke at church synods.

OTHER SAINTS • CECILIUS • SEIRIOL

2

JEANNE DE LESTONNAC
Founder b.1556, d.1640

Home was a source of constant tension for Jeanne because her Calvinist mother insulted Jeanne's Catholic beliefs. Fortunately, her happy marriage to the Baron Gaston de Montferrant created the peaceful home she'd longed for. After he died in 1597 and her four children were grown, she searched for a spiritual vocation with the Cistercians and nursed plague victims before she met two priests who helped her found an order of teachers. Despite the order's success, Jeanne's bishop believed slander manufactured against her by one of her nuns, Blanche Herve, and he put Blanche in charge of the order. Blanche then abused Jeanne emotionally, verbally, and even physically. Jeanne bore this torment with such unnerving patience that it eventually shamed Blanche into repentance. Jeanne's last years were spent in peace.

OTHER SAINTS • THEOPHANE VÉNARD

3

BLAISE
Bishop and martyr d.316?

The Blessing of the Throats, which is associated with St Blaise's feast day, apparently developed from a legend that he healed a boy with a fishbone stuck in his throat. It is believed that Blaise was a bishop of Sebastea in Armenia and was martyred under the reign of Licinius in the early fourth century. Legends relate that, when persecution of Christians broke out in that century, he was ordered by God to escape to the hills. He lived in a cave surrounded by wild animals that came to him to be healed and blessed. After being captured by hunters, he was imprisoned and starved. A woman whose pig he had saved from a wolf on his way to prison brought him food and candles. He was eventually tortured and beheaded for the faith.

OTHER SAINTS • ANSKAR • MARGARET OF ENGLAND

4

JOHN DE BRITTO
Jesuit missionary and martyr b.1647, d.1693

As a page and friend of the future king, John had a great future at the Portuguese court. But John's dream lay in India as a Jesuit missionary. In India, John adopted the yellow robes and austere lifestyle of a Hindu sect so the caste-conscious Indians would recognize him as someone with a message about holiness and faith. Despite being tortured and imprisoned during persecution of Christians, John continued to preach and instruct, baptizing 2000 in one month in Madura. But when John told a Maravan prince that, as a Christian, he must be monogamous, one of the prince's discarded wives begged her uncle, a rajah, for revenge. The homes of Christian converts were burned and their property was confiscated. John was arrested and executed after writing from prison that death was the greatest reward for his labours.

OTHER SAINTS • ANDREW CORSINI • GILBERT OF SEMPRINGHAM

St Blaise once healed a boy that had a fishbone stuck in his throat.

5

AGATHA

Virgin and martyr d. 251?

Although we have evidence that Agatha was venerated at least as far back as the sixth century, the only facts we have about this brave woman are that she was born in Sicily and died a martyr there. In the legend of her life, we are told that she was born into a wealthy and distinguished family. When she was young, she consecrated her life to Christ and resisted any man who wanted to be her husband or lover. One of the particularly determined suitors, Quintian, thought that he could force her to surrender to him by using her Christianity against her. Since he was consul, he had her arrested during a time of Christian persecution and brought before him for judgment. But, when faced with torture and possible death, she simply prayed to Jesus to see into her heart and to make her worthy to overcome evil. Legend tells us that the enraged Quintian confined her to a brothel in an attempt to bully her into

"Agatha...is often depicted carrying her breasts on a plate to represent her suffering for the faith."

acquiescence. But he underestimated her. After she had suffered a month of this humiliation, Agatha never wavered, proclaiming that her freedom came from Christ alone, not from outer circumstances. The heartless ruler then sent her to prison where she was subjected to torture, which included having her breasts cut off. He refused her any medical attention but God nursed her through an encouraging vision of St Peter. When she was tortured again, she died after saying a final prayer to thank the Lord for protecting her from the cradle to the grave, removing her from the world, and giving her endurance to suffer. She then asked him to receive her soul. She is often depicted carrying her breasts on a plate to represent her suffering for the faith. Because Sicilians prayed for her intercession during the eruption of Mount Etna, she is considered a protector against the outbreak of fire. Those suffering from breast diseases, including cancer, also claim the saint as their intercessor.

When Agatha's torturers cut off her breasts God himself nursed her.

6

PAUL MIKI AND COMPANIONS
The martyrs of Japan d.1597–1638

In 1597, the Japanese shogun Hideyoshi, infuriated by the suspicion that Christian missionaries were the advance guard of European conquest, started a violent persecution. Paul Miki, a Japanese Jesuit, was crucified in a mass martyrdom in Nagasaki on February 5, 1597. At first, Hideyoshi's successor showed more tolerance. But, as Christian conversions grew and the first Japanese priests were ordained, he banished all Christians, executing any that remained. Years of persecution culminated in 1638, when Christians were blamed for a revolt and the shogun Bafuku sealed Japan off from the world. But, when Japan was opened up again in 1865, missionaries were welcomed by Christians who had worshipped there secretly for over two centuries.

OTHER SAINTS • AMAND • DOROTHY • MEL • VEDAST

7

LUKE THE WONDERWORKER
Hermit

Growing up in Greece, Luke not only gave his food and clothes to the poor, but also gave them half of his own seed to grow on their land. Determined while still a teenager to dedicate his life to God against his parent's wishes, he journeyed to the border of Hungary to become a hermit. However, he was mistaken for a runaway slave by soldiers and thrown into prison. When he returned home, he received insults for his misadventure. Another attempt to join a monastery in Athens ended when his superior received a vision that Luke's mother needed him. She surrendered to the sincerity of his vocation when he was 18 and Luke spent his life in a hermitage on Mount Joannitsa near Corinth. Also known as Luke the Younger, he is called Thaumaturgus (Wonderworker) because of the miracles God worked through him.

OTHER SAINTS • RICHARD • ROMULAD • RONAN

8

JEROME EMILIANI
Priest and founder b.1481, d.1537

At age 27, Jerome showed no signs of holiness. His world was centred on his own prowess as a soldier and the vulgar pleasures of Venetian army life. But when he found himself a prisoner of war, he decided to review his life. Unhappy with what this revealed, he vowed to let go of worldly attachments. His chains then miraculously fell away and he escaped. After Jerome was ordained a priest, he served victims of the war he'd fought in, opening a home for children orphaned in the conflict and nursing victims of a plague brought on by the ravages of battle. The community he founded, the Clerks Regular of Somascha, established hospitals, orphanages, and a shelter for prostitutes. Jerome died as he lived, catching an illness while caring for others.

OTHER SAINTS • CUTHMAN • ELFLEDA • KEW • STEPHEN OF MURET

9

SABINUS OF CANOSA
Bishop and scholar d.537

Sabinus, Bishop of Canosa, Italy, was a learned man whose studies awoke suspicion in superstitious neighbours who associated scholarship with magic. The pope summoned Sabinus to Rome to answer charges that he was a magician and made him sleep in the hall so he couldn't harm the pope's household. Awakened by music in the night, the pope discovered an angel singing to Sabinus and was immediately convinced of Sabinus's innocence. One charming story relates how Sabinus broke into a sudden grin while he walked in the garden, praying the Office. In the chirps and warbles around him, he heard the birds singing to each other about a wagon that had overturned miles away, spilling corn on the road. The charity the birds showed by flying to tell their companions of this grand feast made him smile.

OTHER SAINTS • APOLLONIA • TEILO

10

SCHOLASTICA

First Benedictine nun b. 480?, d. 543?

The twin sister of St Benedict was a determined woman who chose religious consecration at an early age. After she convinced Benedict to dedicate his own life to God, Scholastica built her abbey near Benedict's Monte Cassino monastery. Each year, they spent one day together discussing divine subjects. On their last visit, Scholastica and Benedict talked on and on, stopping only for a short meal. As daylight disappeared, Benedict rose to leave. When he refused her pleas to stay, Scholastica turned to God and suddenly the house was engulfed in a torrential downpour. Benedict surrendered to God's will and they talked through the night. When Scholastica died a few days later, Benedict cherished the memory of their last conversation – on the joys of heaven.

OTHER SAINTS • TRUMWINE • WILLIAM OF MALAVALLA

11

CAEDMON

Monk and father of English sacred poetry d. 680?

The old cowherd would have laughed if anyone had prophesied that he would become the father of English sacred poetry. Caedmon used to leave parties if he was asked to sing. But then a voice in his dreams commanded him to "sing the beginning of the world." When St Hilda, at the nearby monastery of Whitby, heard Caedmon's dream composition, she assigned him to write verses on doctrine and Scripture. The glorious songs he composed at her request were the first sacred poetry written in native Anglo-Saxon instead of Greek or Latin. After he and his family went to live at Whitby, he translated the whole Bible into Anglo-Saxon. The admiration he received never tarnished his humility. When he lay dying, he ensured that no one had any grievance against him before he accepted his last Eucharist.

OTHER SAINTS • GOBNET • GREGORY II • BENEDICT OF ANIANE

12

MELETIUS

Bishop and patriarch of Antioch d. 381

Bishop Meletius had a sweet, calm nature that could have been mistaken as weakness by those who didn't know him, including the Arians who appointed him the patriarch of Antioch. But at his consecration, Meletius stood up to preach forcefully on the divinity of Christ. An Arian archdeacon put his hand over Meletius's mouth. Undeterred, Meletius held out three fingers, then one finger – to symbolize the Trinity. When the Arian let go of Meletius's mouth to grab his hand, Meletius continued his sermon. Though he was banished by Arian emperors and returned home to find two rivals who claimed to be patriarch in his place, his kindness never wavered. When a mob stoned one magistrate escorting him to exile, Meletius shielded him with his own cloak.

OTHER SAINTS • ETHILWALD

13

ERMENGILD

Queen and abbess d. 703?

Ermengild, the daughter of King Ercombert of Kent and St Sexburga, found herself lifted up no matter how often she sought the humblest place. After she married the King of the Mercians, Wulfhere, in 657, she encouraged Christianity both in the kingdom and her family. Her daughter, St Werburga, entered Ely Abbey, and her son, Coenrad, became a monk. When her husband died in 674, Ermengild put herself under her mother's rule at Minster Abbey. The potential conflict of two former queens, mother and daughter, under one roof, resulted only in both trying to outdo each other in humility and kindness. When her mother left for Ely, Ermengild became abbess of Minster. After a few years she retired to Ely, until Sexburga appointed her abbess there. Grandmother, mother, and daughter were now all together.

OTHER SAINTS • HUNA • MODOMNOC • CATHARINE DEI RICCI

Scholastica's entreaty to God resulted in the miracle of the rain, which gave her more time to spend with her brother Benedict just before she died.

14

VALENTINE
Roman priest and martyr d.269?

We have few facts about this Roman priest, whose name is associated with the romantic holiday. The love that was foremost in his own life was love of God and Christian martyrs. He put his own life in danger trying to comfort martyrs during Claudius II's persecution of Christians. Soon he too was arrested and imprisoned. Tradition says that chains were no obstacle to Valentine's preaching. When he restored the sight of his guard Asterius's daughter, Asterius was converted and had his whole family baptized. Claudius ordered Valentine to be beaten and then beheaded. The association of his feast day with romantic love may have started with the popular belief that birds begin to pair off on St Valentine's Day, first mentioned by Chaucer.

OTHER SAINTS • CONRAN • ZENO OF ROME

15

CLAUDE LA COLUMBIÉRE
Preacher and confessor b.1641, d.1682

Claude used his great gift for preaching to combat the cold, forbidding God of Jansenism. He promoted the Sacred Heart of Jesus to emphasize the warmth of God's love. When Claude became St Mary Margaret Alacoque's confessor, he helped convey to the world her message about the Sacred Heart. When he reached the age that Jesus died, he decided to die more completely to the world. He was appointed as preacher to the Duchess of York but England was still a dangerous place for Catholics. Though many, including Protestants, went to hear him preach, his underground activities instructing converts and encouraging vocations put him in danger. Claude was arrested in the frenzy following the Titus Oates "plot" but King Louis XIV intervened to have him banished to France. He died shortly after returning home.

OTHER SAINTS • SIGFRID

16

ONESIMUS
Slave d.95?

Onesimus was a Phrygian slave who belonged to Philemon, an influential member of the Christian community in Colossae. After running away from Philemon, Onesimus went to Rome where St Paul, who had converted his master, was imprisoned. Later, Paul sent a recommendation and a request to Philemon in his eponymous epistle. Although we don't know how Onesimus met up with Paul, Paul said that Onesimus had become his child in prison. Onesimus was probably not Philemon's best servant because Paul mentions that Onesimus had been useless to Philemon before. But, since spending time with Paul, he had become useful – a play on Onesimus's name, which means "profitable." Onesimus converted to Christianity and became more than a slave – a brother in Christ. And, beyond that, he was an exemplary Christian, serving Paul so well that Paul referred to him as his "own heart". But as valuable as Onesimus was, and as free as he was in Christ, he still owed an

"...he was an exemplary Christian, serving Paul so well that

Paul referred to him as his 'own heart'."

obligation to his master Philemon. It's possible that Onesimus stole money or property from Philemon, because Paul exhorted Philemon to charge him with anything that Onesimus owed. Paul sent Onesimus back to Philemon, with the hope that Philemon would welcome him as he would Paul and then set him free so he could return to Paul. Apparently, Philemon must have fulfilled this request because Onesimus is listed as one of the Christians bearing Paul's epistles to the Colossians. After that, we have no scriptural evidence of Onesimus's fate. St Jerome says that he became a preacher of the gospel and bishop. The Greeks believe he died a martyr in the persecution of Christians under Domitian. Some traditions have linked this particular Onesimus with the bishop of Ephesus of the same name, who was referred to by St Ignatius of Antioch, but there is no solid evidence to support this viewpoint.

OTHER SAINTS • JULIANA

St Valentine's whole life revealed his deep love of God.

— 17 —

ALEXIS FALCONIERI
Co-founder of the Servites d.1310

It seemed impossible to find peace in a Florence torn apart by political bloodshed. But when Alexis joined the Laudesi, a religious confraternity whose name meant "Praisers," he found six friends who shared his desire for holiness: Bonfiglio Monaldi, Benedict dell'Antella, Bartholomew Amidei, Ricovero Uguccione, Gerardino Sostegni, and John Buonagiunta. Seeking a contemplative life, they withdrew to the wilderness on Monte Senario where they formed the community known as the Servants of Mary, or the Servites. Of the seven, Alexis alone refused ordination, out of humility. Instead, he performed menial tasks, even begging for alms. He died on February 17, the only founder who lived to see the Order approved officially.

OTHER SAINTS • FINAN OF LINDISFARNE • FINTAN OF CLONENAGH

— 18 —

THEOTONIUS
Priest and monk b.1086, d.1166

Although Theotonius gained fame for his preaching while he was pastor of Viseu in Portugal, he resigned his parish and journeyed to the Holy Land. After his return he continued to work in Viseu, although he rejected all the efforts there were to appoint him bishop. He believed that exactness in worship was vital and had no fear of those in power. When the Queen of Portugal asked him to shorten Mass, he replied that he was offering Mass in honour of a ruler that was far greater than she or any other sovereign on the earth, and she could stay or go as she pleased during it. He spent the last part of his life in a Coimbra monastery. When he was appointed prior, he never allowed the saying of the Office to be hurried because he felt it would garble the meaning of the prayers.

OTHER SAINTS • COLMAN OF LINDISFARNE

— 19 —

BARBATUS of BENEVENTO
Bishop b.612?, d.682

The life of this pastor is a reminder that sometimes even Christians need to be converted, so that their actions match their beliefs. Barbatus was a priest serving the people of Benevento, about 36 miles from Naples. Although they called themselves Christians, they had never really let go of their favourite superstitions or pagan practices. As a conscientious Christian, Barbatus was horrified as he watched his people worship a sacred tree and a gold statue shaped like a snake, trusting these idols to protect them and provide for them. He couldn't appeal to their ruler, the Lombard Duke Romuald, because Romuald was an Arian who didn't believe in the divinity of Christ, and who was directly opposed to Barbatus's orthodoxy. Although Barbatus continued preaching and instructing, the people of Benevento refused to heed him until he prophesied that the army of Emperor Constans II would lay siege to Benevento in 663. When his prophecy was fulfilled, the citizens realized that

> *"...his life still speaks to Christians across the centuries, emphasizing that superstition is not compatible with Christian faith..."*

their protection lay in the one true God and they renounced their superstitions. Barbatus's next prophecy, that the siege would be lifted, also came true, confirming their trust in God. As a symbol of his victory, he cut down the sacred tree and melted the golden snake into a chalice and paten to be used on the altar. He was consecrated bishop in 663 and used this position to combat superstition among Christians with even more vigour and authority. In 680, Barbatus attended the council held by Pope Agatho at Rome and then, in 681, participated in the sixth general council in Constantinople. He died when he was about 70 years old, but his life still speaks to Christians across the centuries, emphasizing that superstition is not compatible with Christian faith and that all Christians should work diligently to remove dependence on anything but God in their lives.

Alexis Faconieri was a humble founder of the Servites.

❖ 20 ❖

ELEUTHERIUS OF TOURNAI
Bishop b. 457?, d. 532

In 484, the governor of Tournai banished Christians from the city. Eleutherius fled and formed a community for Christian refugees called Blandinum. As more Christians went there, they requested a bishop and Eleutherius was consecrated in 487 as the second bishop of Tournai. Even after Eleutherius healed his daughter, the governor refused to let Christians return and even blamed Eleutherius for a plague. After being imprisoned and beaten, Eleutherius escaped to Blandinum. Finally the governor, believing the plague was God's punishment, called him back. The day he returned to the city, September 22, is still celebrated in Tournai. Eleutherius died when attacked outside his church by Arians who were angered by his support of orthodoxy.

OTHER SAINTS • WULFRIC • EUSTOCHIUM CALAFATO

❖ 21 ❖

PETER DAMIAN
Bishop, Benedictine priest, and Doctor of the Church b. 1007, d. 1072

This Doctor of the Church burned with reforming zeal. Peter's brother, Damian, rescued him from another brother who mistreated him when he was an orphan. Peter imitated his hero, adopting his name and becoming a Benedictine monk. Peter's virtue and learning led to his appointment as bishop of Ostia in 1057. He used his eloquence to right wrongs as he argued against simony and clerical marriage at synods, pushed for monastic reform, and fought against imperial intervention in papal elections. But Peter often inflamed issues with his angry words and, in 1061, he retired to a monastery. Though this didn't diminish his drive it did temper his words, and the pope was able to send him on delicate missions; to settle disagreements among French clergy and convince the German king not to divorce his wife.

OTHER SAINTS • FRUCTUOUSUS

St Eleutherius of Tournai blesses the devout.

22

MARGARET OF CORTONA
Franciscan penitent b.1247, d.1297

Turned out of her father's house in Tuscany when she was 12 years old, Margaret was easily seduced by a 14-year-old aristocrat. After living with Arsenio for nine years and bearing him a son, she discovered his murdered corpse in the woods. Believing this was God's judgment, she gave away all her possessions, dressed in old clothes, and took her son to Cortona. It took three years of extreme penance, fasting, prayer, and ministering to the sick and poor to convince the Franciscans she was sincere enough to be admitted as a tertiary. When Christ told her that the graces she received in prayer were not for her alone, she inaugurated a new mission to convert sinners. Her son eventually became a monk.

23

POLYCARP
Bishop and martyr b.70?, d.156?

Polycarp, who had learned about Jesus from St John the Evangelist, faced the new challenges that arose after all the Apostles were gone. As bishop of Smyrna, Polycarp was immovable in the face of heresy yet was respectful of the disagreements between true Christians, such as what the date of Easter should be. During the persecution of Christians, his community persuaded him to hide at a farm. When officials located him by torturing two boys, the 86-year-old bishop fed his captors a meal and asked them for time to pray before being taken to the arena for execution. At the arena, the proconsul begged him to change his mind and renounce Christianity. Polycarp replied that changing his mind from better to worse was not a change that Christians were allowed. When the fire failed to burn Polycarp, he was beheaded.

OTHER SAINTS · JURMIN · MILBURGA · WILLIGIS

24

MONTANUS, LUCIUS, JULIUS, AND COMPANIONS
African martyrs d.259

These 10 African martyrs wrote a letter from prison explaining that, as they endured suffering and probable execution, their unity as Christians was of primary importance. Clergy and lay people had been arrested when the procurator of Carthage blamed a failed insurrection on Christians. Chained, hungry, and thirsty, the Christians found peace in prayer and supporting each other. One prisoner, Flavian, gave the little food he received to the others. Several members of the group were granted visions that promised eternal reward. Outsiders smuggled in food and the Eucharist for them. Their unity of spirit provided strength in their suffering. Their letter speaks of the shared spirit that cemented them together in prayer, conversation, and action. The community believed that it was impossible to receive eternal glory unless they preserved union and peace with all their brothers and sisters. But the living

> *"Their letter speaks of the shared spirit that cemented them together in prayer, conversation, and action."*

conditions strained these ties. When Julius admitted a prisoner to their group whom Montanus felt did not belong, Montanus harboured a grudge until he had a dream in which he and his companions became so transparent that what was within their hearts became visible. Inside himself, Montanus saw the dark, cold mass of his hostility. Immediately upon waking he reconciled with Julius and the community was united again. Flavian was released, despite his protest, because only clergy were condemned and friends had testified that Flavian was a layman. The rest were executed. Montanus died proclaiming that the number of people willing to die for Christianity proved it was the true church. Lucius and Julius prayed for peace. Flavian convinced the governor he was a deacon and was martyred two days later, praying for unity and peace among Christians – the vision they had fulfilled together under extreme conditions.

25

WALBURGA
Abbess b.710?, d.779

Walburga was a natural choice when St Boniface requested English nuns to help stabilize the newly evangelized Germany in 750. Her brothers, Sts Willibald and Wunibald, had already gone there with her uncle, St Boniface, the Apostle of Germany. As hard as it was to leave her native country for an unknown land, Walburga had abandoned a secure future in her powerful West Saxon family years before to take the veil at Wimbourne in Dorsetshire. After two years in Mainz studying and practicing medicine, she was appointed abbess at the double monastery of Heidenheim founded by her brothers. When her brother Wunibald, abbot of the monks, died in 760, Willibald, now Bishop of Eichstadt, put her in charge of the monks as well as the nuns.

OTHER SAINTS • ETHELBERT OF KENT

26

PORPHYRIUS
Bishop b.347?, d.420

In 395, Porphyrius was asked to go to Caesarea by the archbishop who said he needed help unravelling some scriptural questions. Porphyrius must have sensed there was more to the request because he took one last tour of the beloved holy places he had visited daily while in Jerusalem. When Porphyrius reached Caesarea, he was held down while the archbishop forcibly consecrated him bishop of Gaza. The archbishop knew that the former monk, pilgrim, and hermit was just what the pagan city of Gaza needed. The hostile pagans disagreed and barricaded the roads to Gaza. But, when Porphyrius's prayer ended a drought, many pagans sought instruction in Christianity. Angered by his success, others set fire to his house. Porphyrius, never forgetting his primary mission, converted the girl who hid him from the mob.

27

GABRIEL POSSENTI
Passionist priest b.1838, d.1862

Gabriel Possenti was a ladies' man who was engaged to two girls at once. In his hometown of Spoleto, he grew up to be a quick-tempered, fashion-loving, and popular adolescent with a cheerfulness that characterized his whole life. He resisted a religious vocation almost to death. Two illnesses prompted vows to enter religious life – vows that were forgotten as soon as he recovered. The shock of his sister's death finally pushed him to enter the Passionists in 1856. He found holiness in performing the small everyday acts of charity and prayer with a considerate and cheerful attitude. When he fell ill with tuberculosis, he embraced the new challenge of learning to be patient in his suffering. He died at the age of 24 after, unfortunately, destroying notes on his spiritual life.

OTHER SAINTS • ALNOTH • LEANDER

28

ROMANUS of CONDAT
Abbot d.460?

At the age of 35, Romanus journeyed to the Jura mountains, between Switzerland and France, with everything he needed for a hermit's life: tools, seed, Cassian's *Fathers of the Desert*, and a vocation to solitary communion with God. Three steep precipices enclosed his chosen hermitage under giant firs. But he wasn't alone long. Soon, he had so many disciples that he complained he didn't have room to lie down. So he and his brother, St Lupicinus, built the monastery of Condat in that mountain sanctuary. Romanus was a perceptive and sensible abbot. When Lupicinus alienated 12 monks with his strictness, Romanus told him it would have been better if he'd never come rather than be the cause of driving men from their vocation. Romanus brought the monks back and all 12 became superiors of abbeys.

OTHER SAINTS • OSWALD OF WORCESTER

When Porphyrius's prayer ended a drought, many people sought instruction in Christianity.

1

DAVID OF WALES
Archbishop and patron of Wales d.600?

This patron of Wales studied holiness first with his mother, St Non, and then during 10 years with St Paulinus. He returned to his birthplace to found his first monastery, later replaced by St David's Cathedral. After building monasteries throughout Wales, he settled in southwest Wales at Mynyw. His austere life included hard manual labour, sustained only by water, bread, leeks, and salt. He and his disciples prayed continually and avoided unnecessary conversation. Legend says that when David got up to speak at a clamorous synod, a hill grew under his feet to raise him over the crowd and his voice rang out like a silver trumpet. After serving as archbishop of the Cambrian Church, he died exhorting his disciples to do as they had seen him do.

OTHER SAINTS • SWITHBERT • RUDESIND

2

CHAD OF LICHFIELD
Bishop and abbot d.672

One of four holy brothers who became priests, Chad left his home in Northumbria to study under St Aidan. After returning to York from Ireland to become abbot of Lastingham, Chad unwittingly became the centre of a controversy. While Prince Alcfrid's choice for bishop of Lichfield, St Wilfrid, was delayed in Paris awaiting consecration, King Oswy appointed Chad in his place. As bishop, Chad travelled on foot through his diocese to instruct people in cottages and castles, in churches and open country. When the new archbishop of Canterbury, St Theodore, arrived in England he decided that Wilfrid was the rightful bishop. Chad replied that he willingly resigned as he never thought himself worthy of the office. Theodore was so impressed by this humble response that he later appointed Chad bishop of Mercia.

OTHER SAINTS • JOAVAN

3

KATHARINE DREXEL
Heiress and missionary b.1858, d.1955

This American heiress and socialite inherited values from her parents worth far more than the vast fortune they left her in 1885. Her childhood included 30 minutes of mental prayer and Mass every day. Her parents, besides donating enormous sums to charity, personally provided medical, financial, and job support to the poor in their own home. Katharine responded to many appeals for aid but the pleas of Bishop Martin Marty for the American Indians touched her personally. After funding schools in the West, she travelled by burro and stagecoach to see for herself the impoverished living conditions and the dignity of the people. In 1887, she made a passionate private appeal to Pope Leo XIII for more missionaries to be sent to the American Indians.

"By the time she died she had spent 12 million dollars of her inheritance to support the Indian missions."

The pope turned her plea back to her: why didn't she become a missionary? Missionary work to the Indians was a universe away from her socialite upbringing or the contemplative life she dreamed of. Her friends argued that she could help more people through her society connections than as a missionary. But the pope's challenge could not be denied. In 1891 she gathered the first members of the Sisters of the Blessed Sacrament in her family's summerhouse to serve all peoples of colour. Over the next 50 years she and her order braved harassment by segregationists to found Xavier University in New Orleans, one of the first teaching colleges to admit students of colour, as well as more than 60 Indian missions and schools, and 50 schools for African Americans in 13 states. In 1935, a severe heart attack changed the direction of her life. Although she continued to visit her missions and schools, she concentrated on her spiritual labours in prayer and contemplation. By the time she died she had spent 12 million dollars of her inheritance to support the Indian missions.

OTHER SAINTS • NON • WINWALOE • CUNEGUND • MARINUS

Although shown here dressed in finery, Chad was no stranger to the outdoors, travelling to cottages to meet the people under his care.

4

CASIMIR of POLAND

Prince b.1469, d.1483

The patron of Poland and Lithuania was torn between obedience to his father, King Casimir IV, and his Father in heaven. Despite pressure from the king, Casimir dedicated his loyalty to the true sovereign. He lived austerely and spent his nights in prayer. His father used Casimir's sense of obedience to coerce him into leading an army to conquer Hungary. Casimir turned back, convinced that the invasion was against his heavenly Father's commandments. Though his officers and the pope supported the prince, his father banished Casimir. Exile only strengthened his commitment and he refused to cooperate with his father's schemes, devoting himself to prayer, study, and helping the poor until he died at the age of 23 from lung disease.

OTHER SAINTS • ADRIAN OF MAY • OWIN

5

EUSEBIUS of CREMONA

Abbot d.423

When Eusebius met St Jerome on a visit to Rome they formed a lifelong friendship, shown by the many works that Jerome dedicated to him. Eusebius eagerly accompanied Jerome to the Holy Land with Jerome's other close friend, St Paula, and her daughter St Eusochium. The four companions toured holy places in Palestine and Egypt before settling in Bethlehem. After seeing numbers of pilgrims in desperate straits, the companions decided to build a hostel for poor travellers. Eusebius, the fundraiser for the venture, returned to Cremona to sell his property and then went to Rome to liquidate Paula's possessions. Like Jerome, Eusebius was appointed abbot of Bethlehem and got into acrimonious disputes over the writings of Origen. In the year 400 he returned to Italy and spent his remaining years in his hometown of Cremona.

OTHER SAINTS • CIARAN OF SAIGHIR • PIRAN

6

COLETTE

Franciscan nun and reformer b.1381, d.1447

After her parents died when she was 17, Colette gave away her possessions and became a Franciscan tertiary. While living in a hermitage attached to a church for four years, she resisted visions that directed her to leave her solitude to reform the Poor Clares who had strayed from the life of holy poverty of their founder, St Clare of Assisi. Finally, donning a habit made of patches, she walked barefoot to get the approval of the pope. Though he gave her charge over any convents she could reform or found, she met with hostility. But her loving response to accusations, which included fanaticism and witchcraft, won people's hearts. By the time she died at 67, she had founded 17 convents in France, Savoy, and Flanders, and reformed many others.

OTHER SAINTS • BALDRED AND BILLFRITH • CHRODEGANG

7

PERPETUA and FELICITY

Mothers and martyrs of Carthage d.203

During Septimus's persecution of Christians in the year 203, two African women of Carthage were arrested – Perpetua, 22-year-old mother of a baby son, and Felicity, a slave who was eight months pregnant. The dark, suffocating dungeon "suddenly became a palace" for Perpetua when she was allowed to see her baby son. Despite the pain of being forced to leave her son, and the violent attacks from her grieving father, Perpetua refused to renounce her faith. Two days before their execution, Felicity gave birth to a baby girl after a painful labour. When the guards told her worse pain waited for her in the arena, she responded that then she would be suffering for God. Perpetua and Felicity stood side by side in the arena as rabid beasts were set on them and three other catechumens.

OTHER SAINTS • EOSTERWINE

Perpetua and Felicity with Vincenzo have here been depicted carrying crowns, which symbolize their martyrdom.

8

JOHN OF GOD
Founder of the Hospitallers b.1495, d.1550

The founder of the Hospitallers, John of God never passed someone in need without trying to help, no matter what the cost. When he was serving as a soldier for Spain in the war against the French and the Turks, he was thrown from a horse in the midst of battle. Fearing capture or death, he swore to change his life if he survived. He kept that vow and was on his way to Africa to ransom Christian captives when he saw a weeping family waiting for a ship. Discovering that they were being exiled to Africa for political reasons, he volunteered to accompany them and serve them. After supporting them through illness and financial difficulties, he returned to Spain when they were pardoned. In Gibraltar he became a book peddler to share his love of religious books with others and eventually opened a bookshop in Granada. A sermon on repentance by John Avila, a famed preacher visiting the area, sparked such

"John could never be a bystander when someone cried for help and he died after trying to rescue a boy who fell into a raging river."

a sense of his own sinfulness that he ran through the streets, tearing his hair out, and had to be hospitalized. When he noticed the suffering of those around him in the hospital, he got out of bed immediately to care for the other patients. After he was released from the hospital, he took food and comfort to the poor living in abandoned buildings and under bridges. Thus his first hospital was actually the streets of Granada. When he was finally able to rent a house, he carried his patients in from the streets on his own shoulders. Accused of pampering troublemakers, he responded that the only bad character in his hospital was himself. When the Royal Hospital was on fire, everyone stood by watching – except for John. He rushed into the blazing building and rescued the patients. John could never be a bystander when someone cried for help and he died after trying to rescue a boy who fell into a raging river.

OTHER SAINTS • DUTHAC • FELIX OF DUNWICH • SENAN

9

FRANCES OF ROME
Benedictine nun and healer b.1384, d.1440

Frances dreaded her arranged marriage so much that she suffered a nervous collapse. But with God's guidance she became a loving wife to Lorenzo and mother of two sons, Battista and Evangelista, and a daughter, Agnes. In her sister-in-law, Vanozza, Frances found a companion for her charity to the poor. When civil war rocked Rome, Lorenzo was banished, Battista taken hostage, and Evangelista died in the plague. Instead of surrendering to tragedy, Frances turned her demolished house into a hospital and homeless shelter. When Agnes died Frances was sent a new companion – an archangel. Frances was elected superior of the Benedictine Oblate community she had founded. As she lay dying, she said her angel beckoned her to follow him.

OTHER SAINTS • CONSTANTINE • FORTY MARTYRS OF SEBASTE

10

JOHN OGILVIE
Jesuit priest and martyr b.1580, d.1615

This son of an important Scottish Presbyterian family carefully sifted through religious discussions he'd heard during his education in France, which led to his conversion to Catholicism and ordination as a Jesuit. While braving persecution to minister to Catholics in his native Scotland, he was betrayed by an informer and charged with the treason of saying Mass. Starved, beaten, tortured, and deprived of sleep, he retained his sense of humour as well as his faith. When someone threatened to burn him in the fire, a shivering John responded that he would welcome it because he was frozen. Though his own jailers swayed public opinion with their stories of John's courage, he was eventually hanged for treason after five months of trials in which he refused to betray other Catholics.

OTHER SAINTS • KESSOG

11

AENGUS
Scholar and biographer of the saints d.824?

Aengus had earned the title of "God's Vassal" for the austerity of his life and his humility. Famous for his learning, he once disguised himself and took a menial job in a monastery to overcome pride. But it was a vision he saw in a church that led to Aengus's greatest mission. After seeing angels singing around a tomb, Aengus discovered the man buried there had only one special distinction – he had honoured the saints every day. Aengus never forgot the reward this stranger had received. He became known as the "Hagiographer," or saints' biographer, for works such as the "Festilogiusm," a hymn invoking the names of saints, the *Martyrology of Tallaght*, oldest of the Irish martyrologies, written with Abbot St Maelruain, and the *Pedigrees of Irish Saints*.

OTHER SAINTS • EULOGIUS OF CORDOBA

12

SERAPHINA OF SAN GEMINIANO
Teenage convalescent b.1238, d.1253

Seraphina, or Santa Fina as she is known in Tuscany, gave half her food to the needy even though her own family was poor. After her father died when she was 10, she herself fell chronically ill. She lay on an oak plank for six years, unable to move because of the pain. She never complained, even when her mother had to leave her alone for hours to go out and work to support them. Fina's serenity never once deserted her. From her plank she worked miracles of healing, which included restoring the sight of a choirboy. When her mother died, Fina was left alone except for one friend, Beldia. After days of neglect, she died at the age of 15. When her body was removed from the plank, the board was covered with white violets that are now known as Santa Fina's flowers.

OTHER SAINTS • ALPHEGE • GREGORY • MURA • PAUL AURELIAN

Seraphina worked miracles of healing, including restoring the sight of a choirboy.

QVI VVLT VENIRE POST ME ABNEGET
SE OET IPSV ET TOLLAT CRVCE SVA S

IMPERATRIX IMPERATOR DVCISSA DVX DVX DVCISSA REGIS ANGLICI REGINA
RICHENZE LOTHARIVS GERTRVDIS HEINRIGVS HEINRICVS MATHILDA FILIA HEINRICI MATHILDA

13

EUPHRASIA
Nun b.380?, d.420

After her husband died, Euphrasia's mother withdrew from the imperial court at Constantinople to a simpler life in Egypt. In Tabensi, Euphrasia begged to join a nearby convent though she was only seven. She happily embraced austerities assigned by the abbess to discourage her from such an adult choice. When the emperor commanded her return to honour a marriage contract, Euphrasia begged him to let her stay in the convent, free her slaves, and sell her possessions to help the poor. The emperor was so moved by her plea that he burst into tears and fulfilled her wishes. Known for her humility, she took on the most menial tasks. When a nun accused her of fasting out of ambition to be abbess, she fell to her knees and begged the nun to pray for her.

OTHER SAINTS • GERALD OF MAYO • MOCHOEMOC

14

MATILDA OF SAXONY
Queen and mother b.895, d.968

Matilda's marriage to Henry, Duke of Saxony, was extraordinarily happy and she bore five children, including St Bruno. When Henry became Germany's king in 919, she remained humble, welcoming any petitioner. After Henry's death, her support of her favourite son, Henry, for the succession over her eldest, Otto, led to war. Realizing her mistake, she helped the brothers reconcile. When they both accused her of embezzling money to support charities, she said that she was glad the brothers were working together, even if it was to harass her. In later years, Otto repented of the rift and left her in charge of his kingdom when he was away. In 965 she retired to convents she had founded. Before she died she gave away everything she owned – even the linen that was to be used as her burial sheet.

The coronation of the humble Henry and Matilda of Saxony.

15

LOUISE DE MARILLAC
Founder of the Daughters of Charity and widow b.1591, d.1660

Louise de Marillac's friendship with St Vincent de Paul began when he helped her overcome spiritual anxiety during her husband's illness and death. Vincent recognized Louise's genius for organization, which he desperately needed for his Confraternities of Charity. These volunteers acted as social workers in French parishes, but lacked cohesion and direction. Louise helped them but noticed that the wealthy volunteers balked at menial tasks, so she started the Daughters of Charity with country women who would embrace any type of work. Despite family problems and illness, she always served others – feeding 15,000 war refugees per day, caring for unwanted babies, opening schools for the poor, ministering to galley prisoners, and founding homes for the elderly.

OTHER SAINTS • LONGINUS • ZACHARIAS • CLEMENT HOFBAUER

16

HERIBERT OF COLOGNE
Bishop and chancellor d.1021

Although Heribert longed to be a simple Benedictine monk, his father wanted a more illustrious clerical career for him. Heribert's learning and wisdom soon put him at the centre of state affairs in Worms as bishop. But because he rejected the pomp of his position, Heribert walked into the city barefoot in December. Although he also served as chancellor to Emperor Otto II, Heribert put his duties as bishop first, preaching, comforting the sick, and helping the poor. Heribert was imprisoned by Otto's successor, Henry II, who questioned Heribert's loyalty. Heribert's humility eventually won Henry's trust and he served as his chancellor for two years. Heribert gave all his income to the poor or the church, and would often sneak out of his official appointments to tend to the sick and needy of his diocese.

OTHER SAINTS • FINAN LOBUR • ABRAHAM KIDUNAIA

17

PATRICK

Bishop and Apostle of Ireland b.390, d.461

While still a teenager, Patrick was kidnapped from his home in England and sold into slavery by Irish raiders. He spent his lonely exile as a shepherd in the Irish hills praying and communing with God. After six years he escaped, trusting God to get him safely home though he faced a 200-mile journey on foot to a ship, then dangerous shipmates, a shipwreck, and starvation. But once back in England, Patrick dreamt the pagan Irish were calling him to go back and teach them the Christian faith. After study abroad and his consecration as bishop, Patrick, patron saint of Ireland, returned to the land that had enslaved him to spend the rest of his days preaching, founding monasteries and churches, and establishing the Christian faith in Irish hearts.

OTHER SAINTS • GERTRUDE OF NIVELLES • JOHN SARKANDER

18

FRA ANGELICO

Friar and artist b.1387, d.1455

Guido di Pietro was already a skilled artist by the time he entered the Dominican monastery at Fiesole in 1407, and took the religious name of Giovanni (though he would one day be known as Fra Angelico, Italian for angelic brother). This great Renaissance painter considered himself a Dominican friar first and artist second, expressing his inner spiritual life through visual art. Giovanni and his brother, Fra Benedetto, began painting miniature illuminations for manuscripts and graduated to altarpieces. Then, in 1438, Giovanni began the seven-year-long project of creating 50 frescoes in the Dominican friary of San Marco in Florence, even painting masterpieces on the walls of the monks' rooms to inspire them in prayer. As word of his talent spread, he was given more commissions, including several from the

Vatican, where his scenes from the lives of St Lawrence and St Stephen can be seen in the chapel of Pope Nicholas. Despite the time-consuming nature of his creative work, he eventually served as the head of his religious order at Fiesole, but later turned down the opportunity to become bishop. Described as simple and holy in Giorgio Vasari's *Lives of the Artists*, which was written a century after Giovanni's death, Fra Angelico believed that in order to model Christ in paint he first had to model Him in his life. He began each painting with earnest prayer and completed the work not with his signature, as most artists do, but with an epigram about Christian life. The elements that are characteristic of his style – the serene mood, noble figures, and brilliant colours that glowed with mystical light – set Giovanni's work apart. St Antoninus said of his work, "No one could paint like that without first having been to heaven."

OTHER SAINTS • CYRIL OF JERUSALEM • FINAN OF ABERDEEN

19

JOSEPH

Foster father of Jesus d. First century

The Scripture passages on Joseph, though few, create a picture of a faithful, loving father. Though descended from King David, he was a carpenter of humble means and could sacrifice only inexpensive birds at Jesus' circumcision. Out of compassion, Joseph decided to divorce Mary quietly when he learned she was pregnant, rather than denounce her publicly. But he responded with unhesitating faith when the angel proclaimed the truth about Jesus. He loved Jesus so much that he fled to Egypt to save him from Herod's wrath and years later searched with great anxiety for him when Jesus became separated from the family and was found in the Temple. Joseph probably died before Jesus entered public ministry. But Scripture remembers him as "a righteous man" (Matthew 1:19).

OTHER SAINTS • ALCMUND

Patrick became the patron saint of Ireland.

20

CUTHBERT OF LINDISFARNE
Bishop and missionary d.687

Cuthbert arrived at Melrose Abbey straight from battle, ready to give up the world. When he caught yellow plague, he was told that the whole monastery was praying for him. Proclaiming it impossible to be ill with so many prayers on his behalf, he jumped out of bed. He became a missionary in his own homeland, travelling to the remote villages where he had once worked as a shepherd and instructing inhabitants in their own dialect. Appointed prior of Lindisfarne after half the monks left in a controversy, he overcame the hostility of the remaining monks with his unflappable serenity. He retired to the island of Farne but had to leave when he became bishop of Lindisfarne in 685. He died from the plague he caught while caring for the sick.

OTHER SAINTS · HERBERT OF DENTWATER · WULFRAM

21

ENDA OF ARRANMORE
Father of Irish monasticism d.530?

Enda was an Irish warrior who was convinced by his sister, the Abbess Fanchea, to give up war in favour of marriage. But the shock of his fiancee's death made Enda withdraw from the world. Whenever he was tempted to return to battle, Fanchea reminded him that he now wore not a royal crown, but the "corona" (tonsure) of Christ. Enda asked his brother-in-law, King Oengus, for the barren, windswept island of Aran to build a monastery. When Oengus begged him to choose better land, Enda replied that Aran was to be the place of his resurrection and that was good enough for him. Considered a father of Irish monasticism, his monasteries were known as the "capital of the Ireland of the Saints" and were home to disciples Sts Kieran of Clonmacnois and Columba of Iona.

OTHER SAINTS · NICHOLAS OF FLUE

The news of St Cuthbert's death was conveyed to the Island of Farne using burning torches.

22

DINA BELANGER
Nun and musician b.1897, d.1929

When Dina Belanger entered the congregation of Jesus and Mary in Canada, she took the name Sister Marie Ste-Cecile of Rome, because her musical gifts as a pianist gave her affinity for the patron of musicians, Cecilia. But Dina's true gift was in the intimacy she achieved with God. Jesus was the love of her life. She felt him by her side and loved to talk with him within her soul while walking down the street. Dina believed that if people understood the treasure of the Eucharist, tabernacles would have to be protected with the strongest walls, for crowds would be clamouring to get close to the Sacrament. She said that communion was her daily bread and the rosary her dessert. She died after a long, painful illness that never dampened her capacity for joy.

23

TORIBIO DE MONGROVEJO
Archbishop b.1538, d.1606

Toribio protested his appointment as the second archbishop of Lima, Peru. As professor of canon law at the University of Salamanca, he argued that church law forbade consecrating a layman. Toribio lost his battle, was ordained, and set sail for the New World when he was 42. The Peru that greeted him was ravaged and oppressed by his fellow Spaniards. He spoke out against these abuses and excommunicated those who refused to listen. Turibio visited all 18,000 square miles of his diocese and studied the Quechua dialects so he could instruct the Peruvians in Christianity. He founded the first seminary in the Americas and, not surprisingly, lobbied for better roads. After falling ill during his travels, he refused to return to Lima, determined not to give up his ministry, and died in the next village.

OTHER SAINTS • GWINEAR

24

CATHERINE OF SWEDEN
Abbess b.1331?, d.1381

Catherine emerged from the shadow of a strong mother to shine on her own. Never a visionary like St Bridget of Sweden, Catherine carved her sanctity out of prayer, self-abnegation, and courageous pursuit of God's will. Though Catherine barely saw her globe-trotting parents as a child, she longed to emulate their devotion to God. When she married Edgard von Kürnen at 13, she convinced him to pattern their days on religious life – fasting, praying, and dressing plainly. But Catherine missed her charismatic mother, reporting that she forgot how to smile after her mother went to Rome in 1349. Edgard, chronically ill but devoted to his wife, encouraged the 19-year-old woman to go to Rome. Her mother contrived to keep Catherine with her though she

"...Catherine carved her sanctity out of prayer, self-abnegation, and courageous pursuit of God's will."

hated her life in Rome, where she reported she was caged like an animal in her house because of her mother's fears for her safety. When Edgard died, Catherine resigned herself to staying in Rome where she devoted herself to prayer, caring for the sick, and instructing people in Christian living. Catherine, who said that people who spread spiteful criticism carried the devil in their tongues, was famous for her kind comments. People who saw Catherine as a pale moon reflecting her mother's light changed their minds after Bridget died. Catherine amazed listeners with her forceful preaching over her mother's coffin. On her journey back to Sweden, she drew crowds to her preaching and earned respect for her courageous confrontation of immoral behaviour. The Bridgettine Order her mother had founded at Vadstena appointed Catherine abbess in 1374 and she used her organizational skills to restore order to the monastery until she was called back to Rome to support Bridget's canonization. Exhausted by work and discouraged by church conflict, she returned to Sweden in 1380, where she died a year later.

OTHER SAINTS • DUNCHAD • HILDELITH • MACARTAN

25

LUCY FILIPPINI
Teacher b.1672, d.1732

Lucy was a young orphan in Tuscany when Cardinal Marcantonio Barbarigo saw her teaching catechism to other children and adults in the square of her hometown. He immediately recognized that her talents for teaching would help him realize his dream of an educational centre for training teachers. He placed her in a convent and supervised her education until she was ready to take her place at his institute. Working with Blessed Rosa Venerini, who was placed in charge of the new institute, Lucy recruited teachers, administered the daily activities of the school, and provided spiritual formation. The children loved Lucy and crowded around her wherever she went, calling her the Maestre Santa (holy schoolmistress). When it was clear that the school was growing too large for two people to handle, a community was formed. Though Lucy and Rose differed over teaching methods, the Maestre Pie, as the institute was called, became more and more dependent on Lucy's leadership and organization skills. When Rosa died, Lucy took over but she

"...children loved Lucy and crowded around her wherever she went, calling her the Maestre Santa (holy schoolmistress)."

struggled with the cardinal's successor, who wanted to put his own stamp on the successful institute. She gladly answered a timely request from the pope to open a Maestre Pie in Rome in 1707. In her final years, funds dried up and some schools had to be closed. She spent three years getting the schools reopened but was unjustly accused of mismanagement because of the problems and had to surrender control of the accounts to the bishop. Maestre Pie is also called, by the Pontifical Institute of the Religious Teachers, Filippini, which is a tribute to Lucy's courage and intelligence. These qualities enabled her to forge the way for centres in the US, England, Brazil, Switzerland, Ethiopia, and India as well as Italy. This indomitable woman definitely earned the title of *donna forte* – strong woman – that she was given.

OTHER SAINTS • ALFWOLD • DISMAS

Lucy helped establish Maestre Pie centres around the world.

26

LUDGER OF MUNSTER
Bishop and missionary b.744?, d.809

The great missionary St Boniface probably never met the young Frieslander boy who heard one of his last sermons, but his dream of a Christian Germany became Ludger's mission too. After education in a German monastery and later in England, Ludger returned to his native Friesland to take up Boniface's legacy. His mission to replace paganism with Christianity, by building churches and spiritually feeding communities, was interrupted by the Saxon invasion. When Germany was safe again, he returned and constructed a monastery that became the town of Munster. When Charlemagne reprimanded Ludger for not responding to a summons while he was praying, Ludger answered that service to God came before service to any man.

OTHER SAINTS • BRAULIO • WILLIAM OF NORWICH

27

JOHN OF EGYPT
Hermit b.304?, d.394

In 1901, an ancient cell was uncovered near Lycopolis. It revealed the habitation of John, who, at age 40, walled himself up in the bedroom, workroom, and oratory carved in rock so that he could be alone with God. This former carpenter had withdrawn from the world at age 25 after finding a hermit that became his mentor. John learned to surrender his will through assignments such as watering a stick daily for a year. After 10 years with his teacher and five years in monasteries, John finally felt ready for the complete surrender of his life. But as the disciples who brought his food spread word of his holiness, he soon had to put aside two days per week to speak with visitors seeking advice. Whether consulted by emperors or beggars, he remained in his humble cell where he died on his knees praying.

OTHER SAINTS • RUPERT

28

TUTILO
Monk and composer d.915

How this giant in physical stature and talent wound up in the famous Benedictine monastery of St Gall in Switzerland is a mystery. Some say he was an Irish monk who stopped there on his way back from Rome and others report he was educated there as a child. The mystery of his origins reveals Tutilo's deep dislike of attention about his life. His humility is striking considering the depth of his genius. Tutilo was an accomplished poet, speaker, architect, painter, sculptor, metal worker, and mechanic, but music was his passion. When King Charles the Fat regretted that Tutilo's genius was hidden from the world in a monastery, he misunderstood completely. Tutilo's talents weren't hidden, they were being used to praise God.

OTHER SAINTS • ALKELDA OF MIDDLEHAM

29

JONAS AND BARACHISIUS
Martyrs d.327

These two brothers were arrested for encouraging Christian martyrs during the persecution of Christians by the Persian King Sapor II. Imprisoned separately to get them to renounce their faith, they were tortured secretly out of fear that their eloquence would convert observers. Their captors tried to convince each brother that the other had given in, a lie neither believed. Jonas responded to the slander that his brother had renounced by replying that he knew that Barachisius had renounced the devil long ago. Jonas was executed after he reminded his persecutors that it was better to sow seed than hoard, and so his life was sown for the life to come. When threatened with mutilation, Barachisius replied that he hadn't created his limbs and wouldn't miss them, so was sent to join his brother at God's side.

OTHER SAINTS • GWYNLLYW AND GWLADYS

30

JOHN CLIMACUS
Hermit, monk, and writer d.649?

This desert saint earned his appellation from his book, still popular in the Eastern Church, called *The Ladder to Paradise*, that developed from his years of experience as hermit and monk, and his study of Scripture and theology. After being accused of loving discussion too much, John kept a self-imposed vow of silence until his own community, missing his wisdom, begged him to speak again. The 30 chapters of his book represent 30 steps to reach religious perfection, from the first rung of renunciation to the final step of faith, hope, and charity. He said laughter and rejoicing were signs of spiritual perfection because without sin there was no need for tears. John was the first advocate of the Jesus Prayer, in which Jesus' name is repeated with each breath.

OTHER SAINTS • ZOSIMUS OF SYRACUSE • LEONARD MURIALDO

31

GUY OF POMPOSA
Abbot d.1046

Guy's parents gave him the best of everything. Showered with his parents' lavish praise, Guy grew vain and self-centred. Then, one day, the preening youth recognized the shallowness of his life and exchanged his fine clothes for rags, to his parents' horror. Guy asked his father if he should marry a bride that was average but easy or one that was exceptional but hard to win. When his father advised the latter choice, Guy explained that the best bride was the religious life. After living under the direction of a hermit, Guy was sent to the abbey of Pomposa, where he eventually became abbot, and his reputation attracted disciples including his father and brother. Guy's humility was so deep that when the archbishop of Ravenna attacked him unjustly, Guy treated him courteously and begged his pardon.

St John Climacus with St John of Damascus and St Arsenias.

1

HUGH OF GRENOBLE
Bishop b.1052, d.1132

Intelligent but shy, this canon of Valence was still a layman when he was chosen bishop of Grenoble in 1080. After he was ordained, he found his new diocese had been degraded spiritually by simony and clerical marriage, and depleted financially by the squandering of church property. Hugh worked stubbornly for spiritual reform by preaching, providing houses for repentant priests, and advocating confession for lay people. He improved the city's roads and bridges, and provided the site for St Bruno's new Carthusian order. Despite his frequent requests, every pope refused to let him resign, saying that Hugh, who was by now sick and elderly, was still more far valuable than any younger man could be.

OTHER SAINTS ✦ AGILBERT ✦ GILBERT OF CAITHNESS ✦ TWEDRIC

2

FRANCIS OF PAOLA
Founder of the Minims b.1416, d.1507

Disillusioned by the worldliness he saw on a pilgrimage to Rome, Francis became a hermit at 15. Within 17 years, a monastery had to be built to accommodate the disciples he attracted. Francis required four vows – penance, charity, humility, and a perpetual Lent to encourage Christians to take Lent more seriously. Francis called his order Minims, least in the kingdom of God, to inspire humility. In 1481, a dying King Louis XI heard of Francis's reputation as miracleworker and convinced the pope to order him to France. When Louis attempted to bribe Francis to heal him, Francis replied that the money should be used to heal the wrongs Louis had committed. He stayed to help Louis prepare for death. Subsequent kings found Francis's advice so valuable that they wouldn't let him leave, and he died in France.

OTHER SAINTS ✦ MARY OF EGYPT

3

RICHARD OF CHICHESTER
Bishop and chancellor b.1197, d.1253

As chancellor of the archbishop of Canterbury, Richard found himself in the middle of the struggle over church rights between St Edmund and King Henry III. Deeply loyal, Richard stayed with St Edmund through his downfall and exile. He was reappointed chancellor by the new archbishop after Edmund's death. Richard found himself the subject of another feud when he, instead of the king's favourite, was elected bishop of Chichester. Henry confiscated the diocesan property and income but Richard executed his duties energetically anyway. When Henry relented under papal order, Richard sold the returned property to help the poor. Richard wrote the prayer, "May I know you more clearly, love you more dearly, and follow you more nearly."

OTHER SAINTS ✦ PANCRAS OF TAORMINA ✦ AGAPE ✦ IRENE ✦ CHIONE

4

BENEDICT THE BLACK
Benedictine monk and hermit b.1526, d.1589

Benedict was born to black Christian slaves in Sicily but was granted freedom by the estate's owner as a reward to his father. Benedict found his opportunity for meditation by becoming a shepherd until a man named Lanza, overhearing Benedict's gentle replies to racial insults, invited him to join a community of hermits. After Lanza died, St Benedict was elected their superior. When Pius IV commanded that the hermits join a religious order, Benedict entered the Franciscans as a lay brother. Though he was illiterate, his wisdom and holiness led to his election as superior of Santa Maria. He was so tactful and wise that no one resented his criticism. He also served as vicar, novice-master, and finally as a cook, patiently listening to the many visitors who came begging his advice, generosity, or healing.

St Francis seeing a vision.

— 5 —

VINCENT FERRER

Dominican theologian and preacher b.1350?, d.1419

In 1399, Vincent, the Spanish son of an Englishman, began a life-long mission to preach and bring renewal in the worldwide church, wandering wherever the Spirit called him. This Dominican theologian, teacher, and preacher had spent five years as papal advisor in Avignon trying to heal the schism caused by two rival popes. When he failed, he directed his energy to the people. Thousands gathered to hear him in France, Switzerland, Italy, and the Netherlands. He collected followers known as the Penitents of Master Vincent who travelled with him. In 1414, he preached on church unity to the Council of Constance, helping to bring an end to the schism. He returned briefly to Spain but died on the mission trail through Normandy and Brittany.

OTHER SAINTS • DERFEL

— 6 —

FLAVIUS MARCELLINUS

Roman judge and martyr d.413

Marcellinus, a Roman tribune, was judge over the Conference of Carthage in 411 to reunite Catholics and Donatists, a violent puritan party. Though Marcellinus acted impartially through the conference, he had to rule against the uncompromising Donatists. He enforced the imperial order to reunite both parties and punished dissenters. In revenge, the Donatists accused Marcellinus and his brother of supporting rebellion. In prison, Marcellinus prayed that God would let him suffer for his sins now rather than at the Final Judgment. St Augustine, who dedicated his *City of God* to his "dear friend Marcellinus," described him as upright in his judgments, patient with his enemies, loyal to his friends, loving to his wife, and sincere in his faith. The brothers were executed without a trial, an action censured by the emperor.

OTHER SAINTS • ELSTAN • IRENAEUS OF SIRMIUM

Vincent Ferrer travelled through Europe, preaching to whoever he encountered.

7

JOHN BAPTIST DE LA SALLE
Founder and educational reformer b.1651, d.1719

This great educational reformer said that if he had known what he was getting into, he would never have undertaken the task. John Baptist was settled comfortably as a cathedral canon, looking forward to an illustrious church career, when Adrien Nyel asked him to help open a school for poor boys in 1679. Over time, John Baptist became more and more involved with the school, even taking the teachers into his home. As he lived with these teachers, he was shocked at what little training they possessed. Determined to turn the teachers into "Christ's ambassadors to the young" he quit his canonry to devote himself full time to their education and equipping. Many of the teachers rebelled at his discipline but those who stayed formed the

"...it should always be remembered that the foundation of his teaching

was the faith and prayer that infused his own life."

nucleus of the Institute of Brothers of the Christian Schools. John Baptist decided that his brothers should not be priests, in order to focus completely on teaching. As John Baptist opened free schools throughout France, he received requests from lay people to be trained in his method. To help them, John Baptist opened the first training college for teachers. John Baptist faced much opposition from secular schoolmasters who thought he was depriving them of their living, from the wealthy who thought it dangerous to educate the poor, and from authorities who couldn't understand why his teachers weren't priests. John Baptist introduced many educational reforms in his schools, including teaching in the vernacular instead of in Latin, teaching by the simultaneous method so that the whole class learned the same lesson at the same time, planned steps of skills that were required for promotion for the next level, and the creation of a school community. But it should always be remembered that the foundation of his teaching was the faith and prayer that infused his own life.

OTHER SAINTS • CELSUS • FINAN CAM • GORAN

8

JULIE BILLIART
Founder of the Sisters of Notre Dame b.1751, d.1816

Though the future founder of the Sisters of Notre Dame suffered paralysis at the age of 22 after witnessing an attack on her father, she continued to teach from her bed. During the French Revolution, she sheltered fugitive priests until she was forced into hiding. With Francoise Blin, she founded the new teaching institute in 1803. When Julie was miraculously cured by prayer, she used her regained health to open 19 schools in the next 12 years. A pioneer in women's religious life, she freed her sisters from enclosure and class differences. She insisted children be taught to think and advocated the teaching of the whole child. Throughout her life she impressed everyone with her intimate union with God and her talent for making others laugh.

9

WALDETRUDE
Wife and mother d.688?

St Bertilia and St Walbert raised their children Waldetrude and Aldegundis to love the spiritual life. Waldetrude married a Maldegar, who, though a courtier, was a kindred spirit who shared her love of prayer and good works. This holy couple raised four holy children – St Landericus, Bishop of Meaux, St Aldetrudis and St Madelberta, both Abbesses of Mabeuge, and St Dentelinus who died aged seven. With Waldetrude's permission, Maldegar became a monk and would one day be venerated as a saint. Though her sister, abbess of Mabeuge, begged her to join her community, Waldetrude wanted a more austere life. In 656, she retired to a tiny house built under her direction. So many people came to ask for her advice that she built the convent of Chateaulieu , which grew into the present town of Mons.

OTHER SAINTS • MADRUN

FULBERT OF CHARTRES
Bishop and chancellor b.952?, d.1029?

This "very little bishop of a very great church," as Fulbert described himself, created an educational centre famous throughout Europe. Fulbert learned the value of education at Reims where he so impressed his teacher Gerbert that he was chosen as his adviser when Gerbert was elected Pope (Sylvester II). Fulbert was appointed chancellor of the Cathedral of Chartres in 1003 where his responsibilities included the cathedral school. Under his guidance, this school became the greatest learning centre in France. He continued teaching even after being consecrated bishop of Chartres in 1007. Fulbert rebuilt the Chartres Cathedral after it burned in 1020. His literary works include 140 epistles and 27 hymns such as "Ye choirs of new Jerusalem."

OTHER SAINTS • BEOCCA AND HETHOR

STANISLAUS
Bishop and martyr b.1030?, d.1079

When Stanislaus became bishop of Cracow, Poland, in 1072, he was generous to the poor but strict with recalcitrant sinners, including the king. Tradition says that Stanislaus stood alone, unsupported by terrified nobles and clergy, when he rebuked King Boleslaus for an immoral life, which included raping and kidnapping women. Stanislaus also took up the cause of mistreated army deserters, begging the king to release them and return their property and children. After the king refused to reform, Stanislaus excommunicated him and the king condemned Stanislaus for treason. When the king's men refused to kill the bishop, the king clubbed Stanislaus to death himself and hacked his body to pieces. The pope forbade the celebration of the sacraments in Poland because of the murder and King Boleslaus was forced to flee the country.

OTHER SAINTS • GUTHLAC

TERESA OF LOS ANDES
Chilean Carmelite nun b.1900, d.1920

The first Chilean to be canonized seemed like an ordinary child – interested in sports and music, friendly, active, and happy, if sometimes hot-tempered. But this "ordinary" child had a deep mystical life. She confided everything to Mary and accepted the pain of appendicitis in memory of Jesus' sufferings. She found active expression of her spirituality in teaching catechism and helping poor children. Attracted by the lives of the Carmelite mystics, she joined the Los Andes Carmel in 1919. The dilapidated convent provided the simplicity that was perfect for her contemplative life. She lived by the belief that holiness consisted of love and began a ministry of writing letters on spiritual matters. She died of typhus, taking her final vows on her deathbed.

OTHER SAINTS • ZENO OF VERONA

MARGARET OF METOLA
Dominican tertiary and healer b.1287, d.1320

Margaret's parents despised their daughter, refusing to see beyond her blindness, hunchback, and deformed legs to the intelligent, active, and loving girl she was. When a trip to a local shrine resulted in no miraculous cures, they abandoned her. The frightened girl was taken in by the poor of the city who soon grew to love the sweet, pious child. Margaret's dream of a religious life seemed to come true when a local convent admitted her. But Margaret's longing for austerity was in conflict with their relaxed lifestyle and she was forced to leave. Margaret found a more suitable vocation as a Dominican tertiary. Her mystical experiences in prayer were balanced by charitable service that included visiting prisoners and teaching children. God gave her the gift of healing others, including curing the eyesight of another tertiary.

OTHER SAINTS • GUINOCH • MARTIN I • CARPUS • PAPYLUS

Stanislaus stood up for what was right, even when it meant rebuking his own king.

14

BÉNÉZET
Bridge builder b.1163?, d.1184

In Bénézet's time, building bridges was considered a work of mercy because so many lost their lives crossing dangerous rivers. In 1177, Bénézet was tending sheep in Savoy when a voice told him to build a bridge over the Rhone at Avignon, a perilous section of the rapid river. Although he had no money or experience, he set out immediately for Avignon where he asked the bishop for permission to start the project. The bishop dismissed him and his idea until tiny Bénézet lifted a huge stone to use as his foundation. Bénézet soon gained support and other workers. After seven years, a good portion of the bridge was constructed but Bénézet did not live to see it completed. He was buried on the bridge, which was finished four years after his death.

OTHER SAINTS • CARADOC • TIBURTIUS AND COMPANIONS

15

DAMIEN DE VEUSTER
Belgian priest and missionary to lepers b.1840, d.1889

After nine years as a missionary of the Fathers of the Sacred Hearts of Jesus and Mary in Hawaii, this Belgian priest volunteered to go to the Molokai leper colony, inhabited by sufferers of Hansen's disease who had been forced into perpetual quarantine. He ministered to their spiritual needs and provided medical care and clothes, built houses, improved facilities, organized choirs and even sports events for his charges. But his greatest gift was his unconditional love for them; he did not shrink from eating with them, playing with their children, tending their wounds, and embracing them. When Damien discovered he had contracted leprosy in 1885, isolation and slander added to his suffering. Before he died, heroic helpers came to continue his mission making him the self-described "happiest missionary" in the world.

OTHER SAINTS • PATERNUS OF WALES • RUADHAN

16

BENEDICT JOSEPH LABRE
Pilgrim b.1748, d.1783

Benedict's life is a reminder that holiness is not a matter of outward appearances but of inner holiness that sometimes only God can see. A love of solitude and contemplation led the oldest of 15 children to believe that he was meant to be a monk. But one religious community after another rejected him as unfit for such a life. Not knowing what path to follow, he started a pilgrimage to Rome in 1770. With each step, his real calling in life became clearer and clearer. He would follow the commands of Jesus, going from city to city without supplies, just as the disciples had, caring not for what he would eat or where, thus living in the world but not being of it. He therefore set out on a life of constant pilgrimage, travelling to various European shrines including those in Loretto, Assisi, and Bari in Italy, Einsiedeln in Switzerland,

"Benedict's life is a reminder that holiness is not a matter of outward appearances but of inner holiness that sometimes only God can see."

Aix-en-Provence in France, and Compostela in Spain. Dressed in ragged clothes, he wore one rosary around his neck and carried another rosary and a crucifix, a breviary, a New Testament, and *The Imitation of Christ*. Just as Jesus had nowhere to rest his head, Benedict slept on the ground. Every step he took on his journey led him deeper into prayer and when he reached a stopping place he would spend whole days in meditation at a shrine. His food came from the trash that people had thrown out or from voluntary gifts; he rarely begged. Money that was put into his hands went quickly out again to help others. His lack of concern for personal hygiene eventually brought him rejection from the world that he desperately desired to help. From 1774 on, he narrowed his pilgrimages to the churches of Rome, where he became known as the "beggar of perpetual adoration." In 1783, worn out by his calling, he collapsed in Santa Maria de Monti and was taken to a nearby home where he died at the age of 35.

OTHER SAINTS • BERNADETTE • PATERNUS OF AVRANCHES

 17

KATERI TEKAKWITHA

Lily of the Mohawks b.1656?, d.1680

The first Native American recognized for holiness by the church was the daughter of a Mohawk warrior of the Turtle clan and a Christian Algonquin captive. When she was four, smallpox devastated her village, located in what is now New York State, leaving her disfigured, visually impaired, and an orphan. While living with her uncle, she became exposed to Christian beliefs through missionaries and was baptized by a Jesuit Jacques de Lamberville in 1676 and given the name Kateri (Catherine). After suffering harassment for her Christian lifestyle, she travelled 200 miles on foot to a community of Christian Native Americans in Canada. She died there three years later, having lived a life dedicated to prayer.

OTHER SAINTS ✦ CLARE OF PISA ✦ DONNAN

18

APOLLONIUS THE APOLOGIST

Senator of Rome and martyr d.185?

In his hunger for wisdom and knowledge, this senator of Rome discovered Christian writings and was converted. Although Emperor Commodius didn't enforce persecution of Christians, the laws hadn't been repealed, and Apollonius was betrayed to the prefect Perennis. The case was referred to the Senate where Apollonius gave an eloquent defence of his faith in debate with Perennis. When Perennis asked him if he was determined to die, Apollonius responded that he enjoyed life but that there was something better – life eternal. When another senator told him his words were an insult to reason, he replied that he had learned to pray, not insult, and that truth appeared to be an insult only to those who didn't understand. He refused to renounce that truth, and, after his legs were crushed, he was beheaded.

OTHER SAINTS ✦ LASERIAN

Kateri Tekakwitha was known as the "Lily of the Mohawks."

19

ALPHEGE

Archbishop of Canterbury and martyr b.954?, d.1012

When Alphege was consecrated bishop of Winchester at the age of 30, he was so concerned about helping the poor that it was said there were no beggars in his diocese. In 994, he promoted peace between England and Norway by arranging a meeting between the two kings and confirming King Olaf. War invaded his life again when the Danes raided Canterbury while he was archbishop. To stop the massacre, he confronted the Danes and offered himself in place of the innocent victims. The Danes demanded a ransom for their important captive. Alphege refused to let anyone raise the money, saying England was too poor. A mob of angry Danes killed him in a drunken frenzy. St Anselm considered him a martyr because he had died for justice.

OTHER SAINTS • LEO IX

20

AGNES OF MONTEPULCIANO

Dominican nun and abbess b.1268?, d.1317

Agnes needed a papal dispensation to become abbess of her convent at Proceno in Tuscany because she was only 15 years old. Since begging her parents to let her become a nun at the age of nine, she had developed a reputation not only for her holiness but also for her good sense. Instead of being overcome by pride when she took up her new position, Agnes led an even more austere life that only increased the graces she received from God and her reputation for holiness. Montepulciano, where she was first professed, offered to build a convent to get her to return to them, a community she put under Dominican rule. When she lay dying at the age of 49, after a painful illness, she told her nuns that she would not lose sight of them and that they would possess her forever.

OTHER SAINTS • CAEDWALLA

21

ANSELM

Archbishop of Canterbury and writer b.1033, d.1109

Driven from his alpine home by an abusive father, Anselm wandered through France until he settled at the monastery of Bec where he devoted his energies to investigating questions about God. His exploration resulted in works such as the *Monologium*, an examination about what reason reveals about the Divine. After the Norman conquest, Anselm won respect in England with his straightforward reasoning. King William Rufus reluctantly appointed Anselm archbishop of Canterbury and then tried to force him to resign, finally refusing to let Anselm back into the country. Anselm spent his exile writing his great work on the incarnation. He returned when Rufus died, though he continued to struggle with Henry I over church rights.

OTHER SAINTS • BEUNO • ETHILWALD • MAELRUBBA

22

THEODORE OF SYKEON

Bishop and healer d.613

The illegitimate son of a prostitute, Theodore discovered a role model in a devout cook who worked in his mother's inn. Theodore found the life of prayer more attractive than his home life, spending nights at a nearby shrine and even trying a hermit's life. After being ordained priest, Theodore founded a monastery to accommodate the disciples and visitors who were attracted to him because of his holiness and miracles; he had a special gift for exorcising demons, who called him "ironeater." As bishop of Anastasiopolis, he blessed his diocese by his example and healing, but felt the tangle of administrative responsibilities were choking his spiritual life. After being attacked by a landlord he reprimanded for oppressive behaviour, Theodore retired to his monastery, but still travelled to villages, dispensing spiritual advice and healing.

St Theodore felt called to be out in the villages, helping people.

23

GEORGE
Martyr and patron of England d. 303?

Churches built as early as the fourth century bear inscriptions to the "victorious martyr" George and he is revered as a popular saint in both Western and Eastern churches, as well as being viewed as a prophet in Islam. George was probably martyred in the city that is now Lod in Israel during the persecution of Christians by Diocletian. Texts from the fifth century say his mother escaped with her son to Palestine after his father was martyred. George entered the military and advanced through the army to the rank of tribune. When Diocletian ordered that all Christians sacrifice to idols, George gave his fortune to the poor and proclaimed his Christian faith. He was tortured repeatedly, recovering so miraculously from his torments that he

"George...is revered as a popular saint in both Western and Eastern

churches, as well as being viewed as a prophet in Islam."

converted thousands. Before he was beheaded, he called down heavenly fire to destroy the pagan temple. The popular story of George slaying a dragon seems to have originated in the Middle Ages and appeared in the 13th century work called *The Golden Legend.* George, a tribune from Cappadoccia, rescued the king's daughter from a dragon terrorizing the town. He promised to kill the dragon if the people of the city would be baptized, and they eagerly complied. This legend may have developed from the epithet "dragon" used for Emperor Diocletian in the earlier stories of George. His popularity in England grew over several centuries in which he was entrusted with the protection of the armies of England. King Richard I chose George as his protector during the Crusades because he was a "knight" who had died for Christianity. In the 14th century, Edward III named St George as the patron of knighthood's Order of the Garter. George's place in English life grew in importance until Pope Benedict XIV named him the official patron saint of England in the 18th century.

OTHER SAINTS • ADALBERT OF PRAGUE

24

FIDELIS OF SIGMARINGEN
Franciscan friar, missionary, and martyr b. 1577, d. 1622

In 1611, a young German named Mark Rey started a law practice in Alsace. Though he earned the appellation "lawyer of the poor," he was discouraged by the corruption he saw around him. When he was offered a bribe, he gave up law to join the Capuchins. His reputation for zealous preaching and his fearless treatment of epidemic victims led him to be named leader of a group of missionaries to Switzerland. Fidelis accepted the mission, and its consequences, knowing the hostility some Protestants held for Catholics. His success in making conversions made him enemies and he was ambushed by a mob who tried to force him to give up his faith. When he refused, they killed him. A minister with the mob was converted by his courage.

OTHER SAINTS • EGBERT • MARIE-EUPHRASE PELLETIER • WILFRID

25

MARK THE EVANGELIST
Gospel writer First century

Early references by Irenaeus and Clement of Alexandria say that Mark was Peter's interpreter and that the gospel he wrote about 70AD records Peter's testimony. Clues in the gospel seem to indicate that Mark was writing for a Greek audience and that he was not a native of Palestine. He has become associated with the "John surnamed Mark" in the book of Acts who accompanied his relative Barnabas and Paul to Antioch but left them in Perga to return to Jerusalem. Paul at first refused to include Mark on later missions, but the breach must have been mended by the time of Paul's first imprisonment in Rome because he mentions that Mark was with him and had been a great help to him (Col 4:10). Tradition states that Mark became bishop of Alexandria but was eventually martyred.

The legend of George slaying a dragon has been popularized since the Middle Ages.

26

STEPHEN OF PERM

Russian bishop and monk b.1340?, d.1396

To this Russian monk, being a missionary meant helping people worship God with their own culture. Stephen believed that every language was created by God and was therefore sacred, so he studied the tongue of the Zyryani or Permyak people, 500 miles northeast of Moscow. Though his parents were Russian, he had been born among the Zyryani. There was no written form of Zyryani so before he translated liturgy and Scriptures, he created an alphabet based on symbols in their folk art. When he began his mission in 1379, he used the magnificence of the liturgy and the beauty of icons he painted himself to attract people. When he was appointed bishop of Perm in 1383, he set up schools to teach his written Zyryani and began training a native clergy.

OTHER SAINTS • CLETUS • RIQUIER

27

ZITA OF LUCCA

Servant b.1218, d.1278

From the time she was 12 years old, Zita worked as a servant in the house of Pagano de Fatinelli in Lucca. She treated her work, no matter how menial, as an assignment from God and an opportunity for prayer. Although she went to Mass daily and prayed most of the night, she believed that any spirituality that shied away from work was false spirituality. Zita was patient in the face of her master's rages and the abuse of fellow servants who resented her. She often gave her own food and bed to beggars, and would walk miles to shrines despite darkness, danger, or rain. Eventually her devotion won over her master and his family and she was given responsibility over the house and children, as well as time to do her charitable works. She eventually died after 48 years of faithful service.

OTHER SAINTS • MACHALUS

28

PETER CHANEL

Marist missionary and martyr b.1803, d.1841

The protomartyr of Oceania had never heard of the South Pacific while he tended sheep in eastern France. A priest helped him get an education that led to ordination in 1827. In his first parish, Peter opened the hearts of the suspicious inhabitants by caring for the sick, inspiring spiritual renewal. He joined the Marists to be a missionary but wound up teaching for five years. In 1836, he was sent to the island of Futuna in the New Hebrides where he again used his kindness towards the sick to win trust while he learned the language. The king became suspicious of European intentions, and, when his own son was baptized, he had Peter killed. But, as Peter predicted, his death did not destroy the faith, because a year later the whole island had converted.

OTHER SAINTS • LOUIS DE MONTFORT • VITALIS

29

CATHERINE OF SIENA

Dominican mystic and Doctor of the Church b.1347, d.1380

When Catherine told her parents she wanted to dedicate her life to God instead of marry, they took away her room so she wouldn't have a place to meditate, and then treated her as a servant so she wouldn't have time to pray. In response Catherine created a secret cell in her mind, where she communed with Jesus. There she found the strength to deal with the abuse of her family until they relented. Catherine retreated to her restored solitude, developing her mystical union with Jesus. When Jesus reminded her of the second of his commandments – to love your neighbour – she was reluctant to listen. Telling her she must walk with both feet, not one, to heaven, he commanded her to go out into the world. Catherine obeyed, becoming a Dominican tertiary, caring for the terminally ill, and helping condemned prisoners prepare for

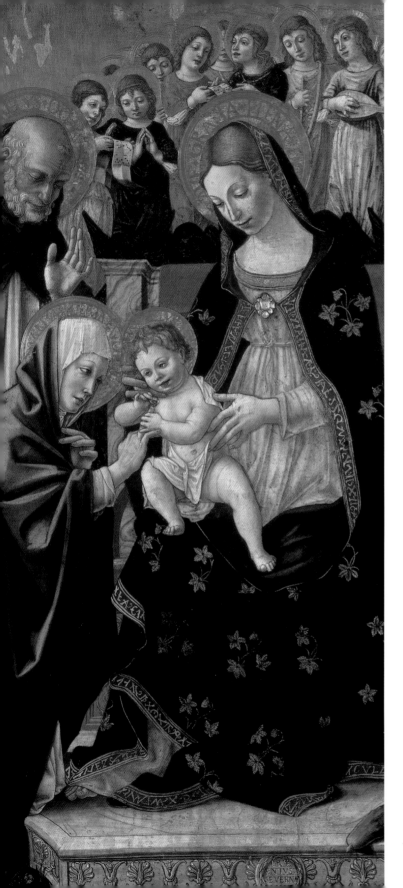

death. When she felt compelled to preach, an occupation that was normally reserved solely for men, she became the object of slander, but so many people went to hear her that four priests were needed to hear all the confessions that resulted. Her mystical life remained the foundation of her activity, even when she entered into public affairs. Through personal visits and letters, she badgered the pope, who had taken residence in Avignon, to return to Rome, which he did in 1376. Several times she endangered her life while trying to repair a rift between Florence and Rome. When two men both claimed to be the pope, she wrote to European rulers begging them to make a resolution that she did not live to see. But her enduring work, and the reason why she was named Doctor of the Church, was her mystical theology, best expressed in her *Dialogue*, a conversation between the soul and God. Worn out by austerities and burned out by the flame of mystical union, she died aged 33.

OTHER SAINTS • HUGH OF CLUNY • PETER THE MARTYR

PIUS V
Pope and Dominican friar b. 1504, d. 1572

This pope believed that he who governs others must first learn to govern himself, something he learned as a Dominican friar. During his time as a friar he realized that by living austerely he could give more money to the poor, allowing him to free monasteries from debt with his frugal administration. After braving stones and beatings to preach to Protestants in Switzerland, he was appointed bishop of Nepi and then cardinal in 1557. Transferred in 1559 to Mondovi, he brought order to the war-torn diocese while living an austere life. In 1566, when he was elected Pope Pius V, he said that without the support of prayer the weight of the papacy would be unendurable. Despite his famous obstinacy, his face shone with such inner light that there were rumours he had converted some just by his look.

OTHER SAINTS • ERKENWALD

Catherine of Siena was called by Jesus to love her neighbour.

1

PEREGRINE LAZIOSI

Servite priest and patron of cancer sufferers b.1260, d.1345

When St Philip Benizi went to Forli on a papal mission to negotiate with the antipapal Ghibellines, he was met by an angry mob. One of the rioters, Peregrine Laziosi, punched Philip in the face. When Philip responded by offering his other cheek, the action changed Peregrine's life. In 1292 he joined the Servite Order and was ordained a priest. Peregrine said he never rested in the pursuit of virtue and tradition relates he didn't sit down for 30 years. After founding a Servite house in Forli, he contracted cancer of the foot. When surgeons decided to amputate the foot, Peregrine placed himself in God's hands. Upon waking the morning before the operation, his cancer had disappeared. For this reason, he is invoked as patron of cancer sufferers.

OTHER SAINTS · ASAPH · BRIOC · CORENTIN

2

ATHANASIUS

Priest and martyr b.295, d.373

Out of the trade centre of Alexandria rose two men whose struggle over the nature of Jesus would define Christianity. An eloquent priest named Arius gave his name to the heresy that Jesus was not the eternal Son of God. Athanasius, consecrated bishop of Alexandria in 328, used his skills as preacher and writer to defend the doctrine that Jesus was truly Son of God. Although Arian beliefs were proclaimed heretical by the Council of Nicea in 325, Arians continued to grow in power, even gaining imperial support. Athanasius was banished and restored several times on the whims of emperors and spent 17 years of his 45-year bishopric in exile, but he never gave up his fight for orthodoxy or lost the love of his people who greeted each return with wild celebration.

OTHER SAINTS · GENNYS · MAFALDA · NICHOLAS HERMANSSON

St Philip always demonstrated his desire to know more of God.

3

PHILIP AND JAMES THE LESSER

Apostles First century

These two apostles, one known for giving Greeks access to Jesus and the other famous as a leader of Jewish Christianity, are celebrated on the same day because a basilica in Rome was dedicated to them both. According to Scripture, Philip was from Bethsaida, the same city as Andrew and Peter. It was probably through them that he was introduced to Jesus. Because Philip's name is Greek, he was probably a Hellenistic Jew, one who had adopted Greek customs. When Jesus called Philip to follow him, Philip responded without hesitation. His first act as a disciple was evangelistic, telling his friend Nathanael that he had found the Messiah that Moses and the prophets wrote about. He dismissed all of Nathanael's objections with the classic missionary

"...Hellenistic Jews went to Philip when they wanted to see Jesus, probably because they felt comfortable with his Greek background..."

invitation, "Come and see" and took the future Apostle to Jesus. The Hellenistic Jews went to Philip when they wanted to see Jesus, probably because they felt comfortable with his Greek background. Philip revealed his own deep desire to know more of God when he asked Jesus at the last supper to show them the Father. After Pentecost, Polycrates says that Philip preached in Phrygia and Hierapolis, where he died. James the Lesser was the son of Alpaeus and the cousin of Jesus that is mentioned in the Gospel of Matthew. A leader of the elders of the church of Jerusalem, he listened intently to Paul's plea that Gentile Christians should not be bound by Jewish law. When Paul had finished stating his viewpoint, James spoke first, indicating his authority on the council. His recommendation that Gentile Christians would not have to become Jews first was agreed to by all and this defined a turning point for the previously Jewish-only sect. Some scholars attribute the Epistle of James to him. According to the Jewish historian Josephus, James died a martyr in 61.

OTHER SAINTS · GLYWYS

4

GODEHARD

Bishop and Benedictine reformer b.961, d.1038

Godehard was 60 years old and ready to retire when the emperor, St Henry, nominated him bishop of Hildesheim in 1021. When he was only 19, Godehard had been appointed provost in charge of the very canons who had once educated him. After ordination, he became a Benedictine monk at Nieder-Altaich. Elected abbot in 996, Godehard was so successful in restoring strict observance to the abbey that St Henry sent him to reform the monasteries of Tegernsee, Hersfeld, and Kremsmunster. So, when Godehard declined the bishopric, saying he was too old, Henry, wisely, did not listen. Godehard worked untiringly; supporting education, building churches, reforming liturgy, and creating a hospice for the sick and poor at St Moritz.

5

HILARY OF ARLES

Bishop and monk b.400, d.449

When St Honoratus begged his relative, Hilary, to join him at his island monastery, Hilary resisted, winning what he later called an unhappy victory. Honoratus announced that he would obtain from God by prayer what Hilary wouldn't give. Within three days, Hilary had changed his mind and arrived at the monastery. Hilary succeeded Honoratus as bishop of Arles when he was only 29, but continued to live like a monk, even performing manual labour and giving any proceeds to the poor. Although an eloquent orator, he was able to tailor his preaching to any audience. He walked everywhere on foot, and used one coat in all weather. His efforts to protect his rights as bishop put him in conflict with Pope Leo, although they evidently reconciled as Pope Leo called him "blessed" after Hilary's death.

OTHER SAINTS • HYRDROC

6

EDBERT OF LINDISFARNE

Bishop d.698

Edbert's life and death were intertwined with his predecessor St Cuthbert. After Cuthbert's death, Edbert was consecrated bishop of Lindisfarne in 688. St Bede's *Ecclesiastical History* describes Edbert as famous for his knowledge of God's Word as well as his obedience to God's commands. He gave one-tenth of everything he owned to the poor and fortified his spirituality with 40-day retreats before Christmas and during Lent. When the body of St Cuthbert was discovered uncorrupt, Edbert had the remains raised in the church for veneration and predicted the space below Cuthbert would not be empty for long. Edbert died soon after and his body was placed beneath Cuthbert's where miracles were ascribed to the intercession of both.

OTHER SAINTS • MARIAN AND JAMES

7

JOHN OF BEVERLY

Teacher, preacher, and scholar d.721

John's service to the poor went beyond impersonal alms giving – he gave people his personal attention. Consecrated bishop of Hexham in 687 and bishop of York in 705, this Yorkshire native ordained St Bede, who tells us that John was an inspiring preacher, learned Biblical scholar, and dedicated teacher. One Lent John took responsibility for a poor boy, who was mute and bald from ringworm. First, John built the youth a cottage and gave him a daily allowance. After his basic needs were supplied, John taught the boy to speak; first the alphabet, then syllables, words, and finally sentences. John also hired a doctor to treat the infested scalp. By the end of Lent, John's charge was attractive, had a fine head of hair, and was so excited about being able to express his thoughts that he talked non-stop!

OTHER SAINTS • LINDHARD

John of Beverly was from York, and was consecrated its bishop in 705.

PETER OF TARENTAISE
Bishop b.1102?, d.1175

In the high alpine pass that was the main route between Savoy and Geneva, any traveller who became ill or trapped without shelter would freeze to death in hours. It was there, in the bleak, frigid wilderness of Tarentaise, that Peter built a refuge for travellers in 1132 and took great pleasure in serving guests personally. Peter had entered the Cistercian Order when he was 20 and he convinced his father and brothers to join him. He was elected bishop of Tarentaise in 1142 to replace a predecessor who had been deposed for mismanagement. Peter put the diocese in order by appointing disciplined priests, recovering church property, and setting up schools and relief for the poor. Peter's famous generosity put him in a hospital more than once when

"...he bravely faced the hostility of his fellow bishops and political leaders to stand up for what he knew was right."

he stripped off his habit in freezing weather to clothe beggars. He built hospices and distributed food during the lean months before harvest. Peter hated the notoriety he regularly received from his generosity and miracles so much that one day he disappeared. After a whole year had passed, he was found serving as a lay brother in a Swiss monastery and he returned to cheering crowds. Just as Peter wasn't afraid to brave the bitter winds of the Alps, he bravely faced the hostility of his fellow bishops and political leaders to stand up for what he knew was right. When two rivals claimed the papal throne, Peter alone supported Alexander III, the rightfully elected pope. Without any fear for his future, he preached his unpopular position in France and Italy, spoke it clearly in church councils, and even confronted the emperor. Gradually, others were forced to admit the justice of his courageous stance. Returning from a mission to reconcile the kings of England and France, he collapsed by a mountain stream and died as he was being carried into a nearby monastery.

OTHER SAINTS • INDRACT • ODGER • VICTOR • WIRO

PACHOMIUS
Monk and Egyptian founder of monasticism b.292?, d.348

This Egyptian founder of Christian monasticism was converted by the kindness Christians showed him when he was a conscript in the Theban army. In the Tabennesi desert, he created the first cenobitic monastery where monks joined in community life instead of living as a group of hermits, as had been practiced before. He divided the community into houses, each of which had a trade to provide support for the monastery and alms for the poor. The monks gathered together for meals and liturgy, and repeated memorized Scripture passages as they performed their tasks. When he died, there were 3000 monks in nine monasteries and two convents for women. St Benedict used Pachomius's rule as the foundation for his own Order.

ANTONINUS OF FLORENCE
Bishop and Dominican friar b.1389, d.1459

This "people's bishop" and "protector of the poor" was given increasing responsibility after entering the Dominicans at 16. When he became bishop of Florence in 1446, Antoninus declared that his wallet belonged to the poor, and when he ran out of money he gave away his furniture and clothes. Antoninus fearlessly cared for the victims of an epidemic in 1448 and rebuilt houses destroyed in the earthquakes of 1453–5. To maintain inner peace, Antoninus said that he kept a secret room in his heart where he retired in the midst of the world's business. He wrote many important works, including the *Summa Moralis*, considered the foundation of modern moral theology. One of his theses of economic morality was that making a profit was not bad if it was the result of working for the greater good.

OTHER SAINTS • CATALD • CONLETH • GORDIAN AND EPIMACHUS

11

IGNATIUS OF LACONI

Capuchin lay brother b.1701, d.1781

Sickly and illiterate, Ignatius seemed an unlikely prospect for the Capuchins in Sicily but he worked hard to prove himself worthy. For almost 20 years, he led a quiet life as cook and weaver, until 1741 when he was given the task of begging for alms. Every day for 40 years, he walked the roads in all kinds of weather, without knowing if the next person who answered his knock would smile or spit at him. Ignatius treated every door as an opportunity to minister to whomever was on the other side. The advice, teaching, and even reconciliation he offered sprang from his years of contemplation and his calm voice and gentle manner made him easy to trust. Soon his visits were so welcome that people even complained if he didn't come begging from them!

OTHER SAINTS • COMGALL • CREDAN • TUDY • MAICUL

12

NEREUS AND ACHILLEUS

Roman martyrs Second century

Everything we know about these martyrs was written by Pope St Damasus in the fourth century on a memorial tablet. According to Damasus, Nereus and Achilleus were Roman soldiers assigned to slaughter Christians. At first Nereus and Achilleus obeyed out of fear for their lives, but they seem to have gotten carried away by bloodlust. Suddenly, a miracle opened their eyes to the truth. They threw down their blood-stained weapons and escaped from their camp, discarding pieces of armour and arms as they ran toward their new life in Christ. As participants in the persecution they knew what awaited them but their victory of faith conquered their fear of death. After they were martyred, they were buried in the cemetery of Domitilla, which explains later legends that they were executed with the great-niece of Emperor Domitian.

OTHER SAINTS • ETHELHARD • FREMUND • PANCRAS OF ROME

The charity of St Antoninus.

13

ANDREW FOURNET

Priest and co-founder b.1752, d.1834

Andrew had no intention of being a priest, which relieved everyone except his mother, for he was an irresponsible youth who refused to study and couldn't hold a job. Finally, no one else would take him except an uncle who was pastor of a poor parish. The example of this uncle inspired Andrew and led him to the priesthood. As parish priest in his home town, Andrew rebuilt his reputation with simplicity and generosity. But he was in trouble again when the French Revolution began persecuting the clergy. Andrew had to minister in hiding, once even evading capture by pretending to be a corpse. After the persecution ended, he worked with St Elizabeth Bichier to found the Daughters of the Cross to teach children and nurse the sick.

OTHER SAINTS • ROBERT BELLARMINE

14

MATTHIAS

Apostle First century

The first thing the Apostles had to do after the ascension of Christ was to find a replacement for Judas. A twelfth Apostle was needed so the Apostles could represent the 12 tribes of the new Israel. In the upper room Peter proposed to the 120 disciples that the new apostle should have been a disciple from the very beginning, someone who could witness to all of Jesus' teachings and resurrection. Since both Matthias and Barsabbas fitted this description, the disciples cast lots in order to discover God's will and Matthias was chosen. That is all Scripture tells us about Matthias. Clement of Alexandria says that Matthias was not chosen by Jesus for what he already was, but for what Jesus foresaw he would become, and tradition says that he became an enthusiastic witness and martyr for the new faith.

OTHER SAINTS • GEMMA GALGANI • MARIA MAZZARELLO

Isidore spent time with people, and often miraculously provided for them.

15

ISIDORE THE FARMER

Farmer and patron of Madrid b.1080?, d.1130?

This patron saint of Madrid and the National Rural Life Conference in the US was a poor farm worker who laboured on the estate of a wealthy landowner of Madrid, John de Vergas. Every day at dawn, Isidore walked to Mass before going on to his place of work. And as he daily ploughed the fields, he turned his thoughts to prayer and union with God. As poor as he was, he often gave his own food to the needy, only eating whatever they left him. His days off were spent visiting shrines and churches with his wife, Maria Torribia. Maria, whose own holiness and virtue matched that of her husband's, was also canonized and is known as Maria de la Cabeza in Spain. They had one son together, who reportedly died at a young age. Isidore's biography, written 150 years after his death, relates that John de Vergas once accused him of arriving late for work because he went to Mass first. Isidore replied that he always

"As poor as he was, he often gave his own food to the needy, only eating whatever they left him."

made up for any time he missed by working more diligently. He promised to pay John back if John evaluated his work and thought he was getting less than his due from him. The story says that when John de Vergas went to the fields to reprimand Isidore for coming back late from Mass, he actually saw an angel ploughing the field. Two other stories demonstrate Isidore's charity. Once, when he was invited to attend the dinner of a local confraternity, he brought along with him a crowd of beggars. When his hosts protested, Isidore promised that there would be plenty of food for all of them. His prediction proved true, either because of a miracle or charity inspired by Isidore's example. Another tale tells how Isidore took pity on a flock of birds that were out looking for food in the snow and he shared half of a sack of precious grain with them. And when the remaining grain was milled it yielded twice the flour it should have.

OTHER SAINTS • BERCHTUN • DYMPNA • EUPHRASIUS • HALLVARD

16

BRENDAN OF CLONFERT
Brendan the Voyager b.484?, d.577?

In the ninth century, an Irish monk in Germany wrote *The Navigation of St Brendan*, retelling the legendary voyage of an Irish abbot that fascinated Europe in the Middle Ages. The real Brendan of Clonfert was said to have ruled 3,000 monks at abbeys he founded throughout Ireland (including Clonfert), and in Scotland, Wales, and Brittany. According to legend, he set off for the Land of Promise to the Saints, a paradise far to the west, with seventeen monks in a coracle outfitted with a sail. During a seven-year voyage through the Atlantic Ocean, he encountered icebergs and volcanoes, as well as creatures from Norse, Greek, and Arabic myth. There is evidence that Irish hermits travelled far and wide, so the tale could be based on a real journey.

OTHER SAINTS · ANDREW BOBOLA · SIMON STOCK

17

PASCHAL BAYLON
Franciscan lay brother b.1540, d.1592

This patron of Eucharistic Congresses and Associations started life as a shepherd in Aragon and taught himself to read and write so that he could recite prayers. When he couldn't attend daily Mass, he knelt in the fields and prayed facing the church. After Paschal became a Franciscan lay brother at the age of 25, he spent every free moment before the Blessed Sacrament. He refused to tell even a "white lie." An errand to Paris took Paschal on a dangerous journey through territory torn by religious conflict. On the way, he suffered many violent attacks, including being stoned by a mob when he steadfastly confirmed the presence of Jesus in the Eucharist. A book of sayings written by Paschal on the Eucharist so astounded a bishop with its holiness that he announced he should burn the rest of his library.

OTHER SAINTS · MADRON

18

JOHN I
Pope d.526

When John I succeeded to the papacy in 523, he was already advanced in age. Born in Tuscany, he had risen in the ranks of Roman clergy to archdeacon before becoming pope. Theodoric the Goth, emperor of the West, was an Arian tolerant of Catholics. He commanded John to go to Constantinople and negotiate religious freedom for Arians being persecuted there. Emperor Justin brought the whole city of Constantinople out to greet John in a candlelit procession and gave him full honours. Accounts of the negotiations are confused although John seems to have been at least mostly successful. But when John returned to Rome, he found a furious Theodoric who believed John had betrayed him. John was thrown into prison where he died.

OTHER SAINTS · ELGIVA · ERIC

19

CRISPIN OF VITERBO
Capuchin friar and healer b.1668, d.1750

Pietro Fioretti was working as a shoemaker when he was inspired to join the Capuchins after seeing some novices walking in procession. Although small and delicate, he took on all the manual work expected of lay brothers. Pietro, who chose to be known by the name of the patron of shoemakers, Crispin, worked as gardener, cook, and in the infirmary in a variety of houses. No matter what the task, his cheerfulness and joy infected all around him. When he begged for alms in Orieto, he became so affectionately regarded that the town refused to open their doors to his successor and his superior had to reappoint Crispin to the position. Important people, including the pope, came to consult with this humble but holy friar. He died in Rome at the age of 82, and left behind him a reputation for miracles, especially healing.

OTHER SAINTS · DUNSTAN · PETER CELESTINE · PUDENTIANA · IVO

St Brendan made a seven-year voyage through the Atlantic in a coracle.

20

BERNARDINE OF SIENA

Franciscan priest, missionary, and preacher b. 1380, d. 1444

This missionary, whom Pius II called "a second Paul," had a voice too weak for preaching when he joined the Franciscans. But Bernardine put all his energy into whatever he did. When he was 20, he exhausted himself caring for plague victims and then nursed an invalid aunt. After she died, he became a Franciscan priest, spending 12 years in prayer and study. Then, in Milan, he found his voice and spoke so convincingly that the crowd wouldn't let him leave. Bernardine criss-crossed Italy on foot, preaching for hours, several times a day. His missions were stopped twice, once by slander and another by his appointment as vicar general, but he was soon back on the road. Even when he was dying, he preached for 50 consecutive days.

OTHER SAINTS • ETHELBERT OF EAST ANGLIA

21

GODRIC OF FINCHALE

Hermit b. 1070?, d. 1170?

Godric spent the first half of his life wandering from place to place, first as peddler, then as a sailor. But even a successful life as a shipowner didn't ease his inner longing, and his wandering feet took him on pilgrimages to Rome and Jerusalem. During his journeys, he met hermits and felt drawn to their solitary life. One day he arrived in Durham, unknown and unheralded. While serving as sexton he memorized the Psalms and sat in on children's classes to learn hymns and prayers. Then he walked into the woods to live as a hermit in a meadow covered with bramble and willow, where he built a wattle chapel. He found a home for his restless heart in God and never wandered again. He wrote several hymns, the first in Middle English, some of which are still in existence today.

OTHER SAINTS • COLLEEN

Bernardine spent many hours each day preaching.

22

RITA OF CASCIA

Wife, mother, and Augustinian nun b. 1381, d. 1457

Rita objected to her arranged marriage to Paolo Ferninando, but his charms soon won her over. Then the nightmare began. Paolo would come home drunk and beat her. He would apologize but then lose his temper again. For 18 years she withstood the abuse and worried as her two sons grew more like their father. Then one night she confronted him about his behaviour. Paolo seemed to be sincere about trying to change but he was murdered soon after this. Rita's childhood longing to be a nun returned and she applied to the Augustinians. They refused her because she wasn't a virgin, but she patiently persisted and was finally admitted two years later. She lived a life of mystical contemplation expressed in service to the sick and spiritual direction.

OTHER SAINTS • HELEN OF CARNAVON • HEMMING

23

JOHN BAPTIST ROSSI

Priest and confessor b. 1698, d. 1764

Anyone who saw John while he was ministering to the homeless, giving religious instruction to cattle drovers, or preaching in prisons, would never have guessed he was afraid. But John had avoided hearing confessions since his ordination in 1721, worried that the strain would bring back the epilepsy he suffered as a student. Finally, he took a chance and learned he had been avoiding his true calling. For John, hearing confessions was the shortest road to heaven because he was helping people get to paradise themselves. He received papal dispensation from praying the Divine Office so he could spend more time with the multitudes that came to confess. John lived so austerely that when he died, he left no money for his burial. Nevertheless, his funeral was magnificent, full of people, great and small, whom he had served.

OTHER SAINTS • WILLIAM OF ROCHESTER • ALEXANDER NEVSKI

LOUIS-ZÉPHIRIN MOREAU
Bishop b.1824, d.1901

Louis-Zéphirin Moreau went to St-Hyacinthe, about 40 miles east of Montreal, in 1852 as secretary to its first bishop, six years after his ordination. 24 years later, he was consecrated himself the fourth bishop of this French-Canadian industrial town. Dedicated to education, he founded Les Soeurs de St Joseph, a community that administered rural schools for children. He built the cathedral, established parishes, and brought the Marists from France. He knew true leadership lay in helping others do their work and looked for ways to give support – financial, intellectual, or spiritual – to those who ministered in his diocese. He ensured that the priests and other ministers knew that he valued their contribution to the benefit of his diocese.

OTHER SAINTS • DAVID OF SCOTLAND • VINCENT OF LERINS

25

MARY MAGDALEN DE' PAZZI
Carmelite nun and mystic b.1566, d.1607

Caterina's mystical experiences began when she was 12 and she looked to the Carmelites to give direction to her remarkable interior life. Though her years as Sister Mary Magdalen at the Carmel in Florence were filled with suffering as well as ecstasy, she insisted that God wanted worship from happy hearts. After making her profession early because of a serious illness, she experienced raptures of union with God. Within a year, however, she sunk into a swamp of depression in which she felt abandoned by God. So intense was her five-year spiritual ordeal that she considered suicide but willed herself to trust in God. In 1590, her winter ended and she began to receive graces again. During the last three years of her life, she suffered physically but used her agony to draw close to God.

OTHER SAINTS • MADELEINE BARAT • GREGORY VII • URBAN

PHILIP NERI
Apostle of Rome b.1515, d.1595

This Apostle of Rome was working in his uncle's business in San Germano when he had a mystical experience that made him lose all interest in a worldly career. He became an urban hermit, living in an attic in Rome, praying and studying to prepare himself for God's plan. One day, he sold all his books and left his reclusive life to set out on a mission to the streets of Rome. His simple method involved speaking to strangers on the street. His charm and sense of humour won people over and when he turned the conversation to spiritual subjects, people opened up about their personal struggles. Soon he saw a need for continuity and organized a small community of poor laymen who met for spiritual exercises and service. After his ordination at the age of 36, large

"His charm and sense of humour won people over and when he turned the conversation to spiritual subjects, people opened up about their personal struggles."

numbers of people were attracted by his preaching and ministry in the confessional. To satisfy these people's longing for spiritual depth, he offered conferences that began with a spiritual reading and discussion, followed by prayer. Each conference ended with a short pilgrimage to a local shrine or church. Poor and rich, aristocrats and labourers, all gathered in the oratory above the nave of San Girolamo. Five of his loyal disciples were ordained several years later and formed the foundation for Philip's new Congregation of the Oratory. Philip's reputation for joy was integral to his apostolate. He used his love of practical jokes to deflate the pride in others and especially in himself. When he felt he was getting too much respect from people, he would cut off half of his beard or play the clown so that people couldn't help but laugh at him. Towards the end of his life, illness confined him to his room but people of all ranks still climbed the stairs to seek his counsel.

OTHER SAINTS • MARIANA PAREDES • PRISCUS

⟶ 27 ⟵

AUGUSTINE OF CANTERBURY
Bishop, missionary, and martyr d.605

Augustine's 40 missionaries to England got as far as France before tales of Saxon violence frightened them into requesting permission to abort. But Pope St Gregory the Great had heard that the Saxon invaders were open to evangelization and was convinced that Augustine, former prior of the abbey of St Andrew, should lead the mission. With Augustine's encouragement, the group went to southern England where King Ethelbert gave them freedom to preach and a place to live. In 597, the king was baptized, Augustine was consecrated bishop of England, and 10,000 of the king's subjects followed him into the church. Augustine tried to unite with the remaining British clergy but differences over the date of Easter kept the churches apart.

OTHER SAINTS • BEDE • JULIUS THE VETERAN • MELANGELL

⟶ 28 ⟵

GERMANUS OF PARIS
Bishop and abbot b.496?, d.576?

Germanus (Germain) was an unwanted child whose mother tried to abort him and whose aunt tried to poison him for his inheritance. He was rescued by an uncle who raised him and had him educated at the monastery of St Symphorian in Autun. Germanus was ordained there and became its abbot. At King Childebert's recommendation, Germanus was consecrated bishop of Paris. He opened his house to beggars who ate at his own table. His example inspired the king to give to the poor and found religious houses. But Childebert's successor, Charibert, was different, and Germanus courageously reprimanded him for his immoral behaviour. When Charibert divorced his wife to live with two sisters, Germanus excommunicated him. Germanus was revered for his power to heal and his concern for prisoners and slaves.

OTHER SAINTS • BERNARD OF AOSTA • GIZUS • LANFRANC

The Madonna and Child appearing to St Philip Neri.

29

SISINNIUS, MARTYRIUS, & ALEXANDER
Martyrs d.397

Sisinnius and the two brothers Martyrius and Alexander were natives of Cappadocia who had gone to Milan to serve St Ambrose. Ambrose was so pleased with their help that he recommended them to his friend St Vigilius of Trent. After ordaining Sisinnius deacon and Martyrius lector, Vigilius sent all three into the Tyrolean Alps to preach the gospel. Sisinnius used a long alpine horn to call the shepherds from the fields to hear the Word of God. Some pagans planned to compel Christian converts to worship in a pagan festival. When the three interfered with this scheme, the pagans beat Sisinnius with his horn and killed him, murdered his companions, and burned each of their bodies. Vigilius built a church on the site of their martyrdom.

30

JOAN OF ARC
Martyr and second patron of France b.1412, d.1431

Joan, born during the Hundred Years' War between France and England, had never known peace. Even during truces, brigands threatened her village of Domremy. Charles VII, the Dauphin, seemed unwilling to defend his right to the French throne against the English who were supported by Burgundy. Despite these troubles, Joan had a normal peasant childhood. Later testimony spoke of Joan's piety and her concern for others but there was nothing to indicate that she would be singled out by God. When she was 14, she started having visions that she identified as saints. Over time they revealed that God had chosen her to save France. Joan resisted the voices for practical reasons, including her lack of military training, but she was told it was God's command. Joan was ignored by the army until she accurately predicted a defeat at Orleans. At court, she convinced the Dauphin of her divine commission by revealing a secret. After a theological panel reviewed her case, Joan rode to Orleans at the head of the French army. Within two days they had defeated the English and secured the city. Despite an arrow wound, Joan cleared the way to Rheims so that the Dauphin could be crowned King of France, with Joan at his side. Joan was captured by the Burgundians the following year at Compiegne. When the French king refused to help her, the Burgundians sold her to the English who tried her for sorcery. Alone and betrayed, she courageously answered the tribunal headed by the ambitious bishop of Beauvais and his handpicked judges. The verdict was a foregone conclusion, however, and she was burned at the stake in Rouen. Twenty-three years later her case was reopened on appeal from her mother and brothers and Joan was declared innocent. She was canonized in 1920.

OTHER SAINTS • HUBERT • FERDINAND

31

MECHTILDIS OF EDELSTETTEN
Abbess b.1125, d.1160

When Mechtildis was 28 years old, the bishop of Augsburg asked her to reform the permissive convent of Edelstetten. The bishop had heard how she had inspired her own community to virtue with her sanctity as abbess. But Mechtildis had been at Diessen on her parents' estate since she was five years old and Edelstetten seemed beyond her limited experience. Only when the pope admonished her that obedience was better than sacrifice did Mechtildis accept the position. Her new community was pleased with the choice, believing that this young noblewoman would sympathize with their preference of pleasure over spirituality. But when Mechtildis cut off society with the world and enforced discipline, her charges rebelled. The most stubborn had to be expelled but Mechtildis's holy life converted the rest.

OTHER SAINTS • PETRONELLA

Joan of Arc entered Orleans at the head of the French army.

1

JUSTIN

Apologist and martyr d.165

After studying in Rome, Justin felt no closer to the truth he'd been searching for. He discarded many schools of philosophy because they didn't lead him to God. Then, while walking on the beach, he encountered an old man who directed him to the Scriptures. From there, Justin was led to Christ's words where he discovered a power that changed his life. At the time Christians kept their beliefs secret out of fear, but Justin believed they had an obligation to speak out. So this layman became the first great apologist for Christianity, using his education to explain why Christians didn't worship idols, why they didn't follow Jewish laws, and why philosophy was not enough. Justin was arrested during the persecution under Marcus Aurelius and beheaded.

OTHER SAINTS • GWEN OF BRITTANY • NICODEMUS • RONAN

2

MARCELLINUS & PETER

Roman martyrs d.304

Pope St Damasus says that he heard the story of these two martyrs from their executioner, Dorotheus, who became a Christian after their deaths. Marcellinus, a priest, and Peter, an exorcist, were arrested after Diocletian proclaimed his edict against Christian clergy. The two Romans saw their imprisonment as an opportunity to evangelize and converted their jailer and his wife and daughter. The jailer and his family were then crushed to death while Marcellinus and Peter were led to the forest and told to clear brambles from the place of their execution. They were beheaded secretly so that their bodies wouldn't be venerated. The executioner, however, divulged the location of the bodies to two Christian women who buried them. Their names appear in the first Eucharistic prayer and Constantine built a basilica over their tomb.

The Madonna and Child with Sts Justin (right) and Clement.

3

CHARLES LWANGA & COMPANIONS

Martyrs of Uganda d.1886

The 22 African Catholic martyrs honoured today were executed by King Mwanga, a paedophile enraged that Christian converts in his court were protecting boy pages from him. The young men, including Charles Lwanga, the leading catechist at court, had been converted to Christianity by the Society of Missionaries of Africa (the White Fathers). In May 1886, after murdering one catechist himself, Mwanga marched the Christians 37 miles, and then those who hadn't died from the long trek were burned. When the White Fathers returned after King Mwanga's death, they found 500 Christians and 1000 catechumens that the Ugandans had instructed secretly in their absence.

OTHER SAINTS • CLOTILDE • GENESIUS OF CLERMONT • KEVIN

4

FRANCIS CARACCIOLO

Co-founder of the Regular Clerks Minor and priest b.1563, d.1608

The path to holiness for Ascanio Caracciolo was a case of mistaken identity. Ascanio led the normal life of a young Neapolitan noble until a repulsive skin disease revealed the futility of worldly vanity. After his skin healed, he was ordained. He developed a special ministry to prisoners. Then he received a letter meant for a different Ascanio Caracciolo. The letter from John Augustine Adorno proposed a new religious order that combined contemplation and action. The idea excited Ascanio who became co-founder of the Regular Clerks Minor, taking the name Francis. He was so humble that when he was appointed superior, he insisted on taking his turn at menial tasks. When people tried to honour him in his home town, he fell on his knees and, holding up a crucifix, shouted, "Look at Him, not me!"

OTHER SAINTS • EDFRITH • NINNOC • PETROC

BONIFACE OF MAINZ
Missionary and martyr d.675

In his mid-40s, Winfrith abandoned a successful life in England as a respected scholar, teacher, and priest because he was convinced he was called to missionary work. But when he got to Friesland (now Holland), the ruler, Radbod, had declared war on Christians, and Winfrith had no choice but to return to England in defeat. Winfrith saw a message in this fiasco but the message was not "Quit" but "Plan." He went to Rome to get official backing and Pope Gregory II sent him on a test mission to Thuringia in Germany, where the church had degraded into superstition and heresy. He went with a new name – Boniface. While Boniface was in Thuringia, he heard that Radbod had died and immediately went to Friesland to get on-the-job training from the great missionary Willibrord. Willibrord wanted to make Boniface his successor but Boniface felt the pull of the German missionary work he'd left behind and went to Hesse, which had never been evangelized. Needing authority to convince chieftains to accept him, he appealed to the pope again and was consecrated bishop. To prove their old beliefs were powerless to protect them, Boniface called the tribes together and cut down the giant oak of Geismar, a sacred tree dedicated to Thor, with an axe. After his success in Hesse, he returned to Thuringia to try to repair the church there and brought nuns and monks over from England to help with the reform. At 73, a time when most think of retirement, Boniface headed back to Friesland on a new mission. One day while he was awaiting some confirmands, enemy tribesman attacked his camp. Although his companions wanted to fight back, Boniface told them to trust in God and welcome death for the faith. All were martyred.

Scenes from Boniface's life show him baptizing believers and being martyred.

6

NORBERT
Bishop b. 1080?, d. 1134

Norbert always chose the easy way in the pleasure-loving German court where he was a canon. Then, when he was thrown from his horse during a lightning storm, he heard God command him to change. After his ordination in 1115, Norbert gave his possessions to the poor and became an itinerant preacher, walking barefoot even in winter. He founded a community in the lonely valley of Prémontré and instituted the first lay affiliation with a religious order when he gave Count Theobald a rule to follow in the world. When Norbert arrived at his new residence after being consecrated bishop of Magdeburg, the porter assumed he was a beggar. The man was mortified as he realized his mistake but Norbert told him he had been right the first time.

OTHER SAINTS • GUDWAL • JARLATH • PRIMUS AND FELICIAN

7

ANNE OF ST BARTHOLOMEW
Carmelite nun and prioress b. 1549, d. 1626

In 1570, this young illiterate shepherdess joined St Teresa of Avila's reformed Carmelites. Anne's shyness couldn't disguise her intelligence and devotion and she became Teresa's constant companion on her arduous journeys. Anne would kneel for hours outside Teresa's cell in case she was needed. After learning to write, she became Teresa's secretary and composed religious verse as well as an autobiography. Anne nursed Teresa during her illnesses and Teresa breathed her last in Anne's arms. Anne seemed destined for a quiet life after that until she was called to Paris to help found a Discalced Carmelite convent. After serving as prioress in the French convents at Pontoise and Tours, she founded a convent in Antwerp in 1612 where she guided the daughters of nobles in holiness and sheltered refugees from English persecution.

OTHER SAINTS • ROBERT OF NEWMINSTER • ANTONIO GIANELLI

8

MEDARD OF VERMANDOIS
Bishop b. 470?, d. 560?

Medard was raised in Salency, France, by a Roman mother and a Frank father, converted to Christianity by his wife. As Medard grew, his piety withstood all temptations. At 33, his reputation convinced Bishop Alomer of Vermandois to ordain him priest. Though Medard had reached an advanced age when he was consecrated as Alomer's successor, he pursued his responsibilities with fervour. Tradition says he released a thief caught stealing grapes from his garden, saying he had given the man the grapes. He supported Queen St Radegund after her husband murdered her brother, consecrated her to religious life, and ordained her as deaconess. He is credited with instituting the Festival of the Rose when the most virtuous girl in Salency is crowned with roses.

9

EPHREM
Composer b. 306?, d. 373?

Ephrem the Syrian is credited with awakening the church to the importance of music and poetry in spreading the faith. His hymns imply that he was born into a Christian family, but not baptized until he was an adult. Ephrem served as teacher, and possibly deacon, at Nisibis in Mesopotamia. Recognizing the power of music to instill a message, Ephrem began to promote orthodoxy and condemn heresy in hymns. After the Persian king forced Christians from Nisibis, Ephrem became a solitary ascetic on Mount Edessa. When the Arian Emperor Valens threatened to kill the Christians in Edessa, Ephrem's hymns were again used to encourage the inhabitants to remain steadfast. During a famine in 372, Ephrem reportedly confronted hoarders and distributed their stockpiled food to the needy. He died shortly after the famine ended.

OTHER SAINTS • COLUMBA

10

LANDRY
Bishop of Paris d.660?

Only one year after Landry was consecrated bishop of Paris in 650, the poor were devastated by famine and epidemic. Desperate to help them, he sold everything he owned to buy food. When that wasn't enough, he sold the cathedral chalices, patens, and furnishings. The only refuges for poor epidemic victims were overcrowded hostels supported by voluntary alms, so Landry conceived the first real hospital in Europe, St Christopher's. Located north of the cathedral of Notre Dame, Landry's hospital lives on as one of the greatest institutions in modern France, the Hôtel-Dieu. Landry also commissioned a monk named Marculf to compile the first French ecclesiastical code, "Recueil de Formules," which is dedicated to him.

OTHER SAINTS ◆ ITHAMAR

11

BARNABAS
Apostle d.60?

Scripture tells us that Barnabas was a good man, filled with the Holy Spirit and faith. Though his name was Joseph, this Levite from Cyprus came to be known by the name Barnabas, which means "son of encouragement or exhortation." As his name implies, Barnabas was fervent in his efforts to win many converts. He also encouraged the Apostles to accept their former persecutor, Paul. After the apostles commissioned Barnabas and Paul to spread the Gospel by the laying on of hands, they travelled together, preaching and founding churches. They eventually parted ways over Paul's distrust of Barnabas's relative, Mark. Later Barnabas went to Cyprus, where tradition says he was martyred. Though not one of the original 12, Barnabas earned the title Apostle because of his special commission for missionary work.

12

JOHN of SAHAGUN
Augustinian priest b.1430, d.1479

John's conscience told him that just because everyone was committing a wrong didn't make it right. To the disgust of his father and the bishop of Burgos, he resigned his illegal plural church offices with their lucrative incomes, keeping only the parish of St Agnes. After studying in Salamanca, and while working as a priest, his reputation for holiness was marred by complaints that he celebrated Mass too slowly. John explained he had a just impediment – he was having mystical experiences during the Mass. He worked to resolve the feuds prevalent at the time and preached so forcefully against oppressing the poor that the Duke of Alba sent assassins after him. But once they saw their holy target the murderers repented, begging forgiveness!

OTHER SAINTS ◆ BASILIDES ◆ ESKIL ◆ LEO II ◆ ODULF

13

ANTHONY of PADUA
Franciscan friar and priest b.1195, d.1231

At 27, Anthony wondered where his life was going. He had left a peaceful life of prayer and study in a Portuguese monastery to become a Franciscan missionary. But the Franciscans recalled him from Morocco when he fell ill shortly after arriving. The Italian Franciscans thought he was too sick even to wash dishes and sent him to a mountain retreat. Then, in 1222, he was ordered to preach to the toughest crowd of all – other priests. Miraculously his studies, his contemplation, and his experiences came together in a magnificent sermon. From then on, he was Anthony the Preacher. He was so popular that businesses closed when he came to town. But Anthony believed that the most important preaching was done by example and made sure that his actions matched every word he spoke.

The popular preacher, St Anthony of Padua.

❖ 14 ❖

METHODIUS OF CONSTANTINOPLE

Patriarch of Constantinople d.847

The iconoclasts condemned images of Christ and saints as superstitious objects to be destroyed. Because Methodius, a Sicilian monk, argued that images were aids to devotion, the iconoclastic emperor in Constantinople imprisoned him in a cramped tomb with two thieves, one of whom died and was left to rot. In these horrifying conditions, Methodius's kindness won the devotion of the other inmate, who remained with him after their release. The orthodox Empress Theodora freed Methodius and he reaffirmed his beliefs during a confrontation with Theodora's iconoclastic husband, Theophilus. Theophilus died soon after and Theodora restored orthodoxy, allowing Methodius to ascend to the throne of the patriarch of Constantinople.

OTHER SAINTS ✦ DOGMAEL

❖ 15 ❖

GERMAINE COUSIN

Shepherdess b.1579, d.1601

Germaine was born with a deformed right hand and may also have been illegitimate. Her family tormented and neglected her, putting ashes in her food and tar in her clothes, making her sleep in the barn, and even pouring boiling water on her legs. Under this abuse, Germaine acquired scrofula, a tuberculosis of the neck glands. As Germaine tended the family sheep, she prayed with a rosary of knotted string. Every day, she left her sheep in God's care so she could go to Mass. Germaine shared what little she had with others, giving her scraps of food to beggars. As the village recognized her holiness, her family's attitude changed and softened and she was invited back to the house. Germaine chose to remain in the barn where she was found dead at age 22.

OTHER SAINTS ✦ TRILLO ✦ VITUS AND COMPANIONS

Lutgard's mystical experiences of Jesus were marked by intimacy, as if she were speaking to a friend instead of praying.

16

LUTGARD
Cistercian nun and mystic b.1182, d.1246

Lutgard, a beloved medieval mystic, was a normal teenager in the Netherlands who liked fashionable clothes, talking with friends, and having a good time. The problem with her lifestyle was that Lutgard was a Benedictine postulant. When she was 12 years old, her father lost her dowry in a business deal. The loss of the dowry meant she could no longer marry. The Middle Ages offered only one other acceptable option – religious life. So Lutgard was taken to St Catherine's, even though she had no religious vocation. The nuns gave her a lot of freedom, allowing her to have outside visitors and leave the convent for short periods of time. Then, one day, a visit with a friend was interrupted by Jesus commanding her to love him only. Lutgard immediately reformed her life. The other nuns were cynical, believing that she would soon return to her old ways. But Lutgard, sustained by further mystical graces,

"She had a supernatural empathy that enabled her to share the spiritual and physical pain of other people."

persisted and was professed when she was 20. Her mystical experiences of Jesus were marked by intimacy, as if she were speaking to a friend instead of praying. She had a supernatural empathy that enabled her to share the spiritual and physical pain of other people. She used this gift to counsel and heal sufferers. Empathy galvanized her intercessory prayer, so that she even offered to exchange her own eternal life for God's mercy on some other soul. Attracted to a stricter rule, she entered the Cistercian convent at Aywières, though the nuns spoke only French and she knew only German. The inability to communicate increased her detachment from the world and kept her humble. She became blind at 53 but welcomed the opportunity to turn her inner vision to God. Eleven years later, Jesus advised her to prepare for death by thanking God for all his gifts, praying constantly for sinners, and trusting in God alone.

OTHER SAINTS • BENNO • CYRICUS • ISMAEL

17

ALBERT CHMIELOWSKI
Franciscan tertiary b.1845, d.1916

Krakow society loved this talented painter who had lost his leg in the war against Russia. But Adam heard the cries of the homeless over flattery of the rich, and became the Franciscan tertiary Brother Albert. He lived in the city's homeless shelter with the poor he served, braving bugs and filth to distribute food and medical care. Over time he renovated the shelter and organized training, retreats, and entertainment. When authorities tried to enforce limitations on his aid, he responded that mercy was more important than rules. When asked if he was happy, Albert laughed and said that his answer lay in the shelters he had built all over Poland, the 20,000 loaves of bread he distributed each year, and the hundreds of souls he sheltered every night.

OTHER SAINTS • ADULF • ALBAN • BOTULF • BRIAVEL

18

HOSANNA OF MANTUA
Dominican tertiary and mystic b.1449, d.1505

Hosanna received her first mystical experience at age five when she was shown the different ways creatures praise God in a vision. From that day she committed her life to God, even teaching herself to read and write so she could learn about her faith. She tricked her reluctant father into letting her become a Dominican tertiary by saying she was donning the habit temporarily and then announcing she had made a commitment. Her mystical experiences, however, excited suspicion among other tertiaries, which may explain why she remained a novice for 37 years. It was her wisdom and practical skills, however, that inspired her relative, the Duke of Mantua, to put her in charge of his family while he was away. She used her influence with him to obtain justice and mercy in various causes.

OTHER SAINTS • MARK • MARCELLIAN • GREGORY BARBARIGO

ROMUALD

Hermit and monk b.951?, d.1027?

Romuald's comfortable life changed in an instant when he saw his father kill a relative in a duel over a piece of land. Horrified, Romuald ran to the nearby monastery St-Apollinare-in-Classe where he dedicated his life to seeking holiness and atoning for the murder. But after three years some monks, resentful of his efforts to increase austerities in the monastery, forced him out. A hermit took Romuald in and guided him even farther down the path of perfection. Romuald then travelled through Italy for 30 years, founding monasteries and hermitages, writing commentaries on the Psalms, and giving advice and direction to spiritual seekers. His example eventually convinced his father to reform his own life and the man spent his last years as a monk.

OTHER SAINTS • GERVASE AND PROTASE • JULIANA FALCONIERI

ALOYSIUS GONZAGA

Jesuit b.1568, d.1591

To outward appearances, this son of the Marquis of Castiglione lived like any other noble youth. From the time he was eight he was placed in one court after another, eventually becoming a page to the Spanish Crown Prince, and dressing in velvets and silks. But inside his desire to live a far different life had grown from the time he was seven. At 11 he'd decided to give his title and his inheritance to his brother and by his early teenage years he'd decided to join the Jesuits. His father was reluctant to let his heir enter the Jesuit novitiate but gave his permission in 1585. Aloysius embraced religious life but his health was always delicate. Nevertheless, he put all his energy into nursing plague victims in Rome until he caught a fever and died.

OTHER SAINTS • LEUFRED • MEWAN

ADALBERT OF MAGDEBURG

Archbishop d.981

In 961, Adalbert, a monk of St-Maximin at Trier, was appointed by the German Emperor Otto III to fulfil the request of Princess Olga of Russia for missionaries to Slavic tribes. But by the time Adalbert approached Kiev, Olga had been forced from power by her son. The missionaries were massacred and Adalbert barely escaped. Otto appointed him abbot of Weissenberg, where he promoted education and contributed to a historical chronicle. In 968, in an effort to fortify his northeastern borders, Otto convinced the pope to create a new archdiocese at Magdeburg and consecrate Adalbert as its first archbishop. Under his rule, Magdeburg became one of the great archdioceses of Germany. But he never forgot his first mission, spending much of his energy on converting the tribes of Wends that lived across the river.

OTHER SAINTS • ALBAN • EDWARD THE MARTYR • GOVAN

Romuald gave blessings and advice to all those who sought him out.

PAULINUS OF NOLA

Bishop and poet b.353, d.431

Paulinus was an accomplished orator and poet whose duties as Roman prefect took him all over Europe where his character, style, and imagination won friends such as Sts Ambrose and Jerome. The miracles that he witnessed at St Felix's tomb in Nola, however, convinced him to dedicate his life to God. After he was baptized, he and his virtuous Spanish wife Therasia retired to Barcelona for four years where their only son died in infancy and Paulinus was forcibly ordained in 393. They sold their possessions and withdrew as hermits to Nola where Paulinus opened his house to homeless debtors. Every year he wrote poetry in honour of St Felix, some of which is still extant. Friends who had criticized him for burying his talents in the past were vindicated by his election as bishop of Nola in 409.

OTHER SAINTS • ACACIUS • JOHN FISHER AND THOMAS MOORE

23

ETHELDREDA

Saxon princess and nun d.679

This Saxon princess of East Anglia was forced to put aside her wishes for religious life to submit to a political marriage to the devoted Prince Tombert. After his death three years later, she escaped like a freed bird to seclusion on the Island of Ely. Her freedom ended with a second political marriage to Egfrid, prince of Northumbria. Egfrid loved his wife but her heart belonged elsewhere. After 12 years, Egfrid agreed to a separation and Etheldreda entered the Coldingham Convent. When Egfrid pursued her, she fled, disguised as a poor woman, to Ely. She exchanged the linen clothing of her rank for rough wool and ruled a double monastery of monks and nuns. Her sanctity was sustained with daily prayer from midnight to daybreak.

OTHER SAINTS • CYNEBURG

24

JOHN THE BAPTIST

Prophet and cousin of Jesus First century

This prophet and Mary are the only saints whose birthdays are celebrated by the church because they were sanctified before birth. The angel Gabriel announced to John's father Zechariah that John would be filled with the Holy Spirit in the womb. John's birth was miraculous, not only because it ended the long childlessness of Zechariah and Elizabeth, but also because angel Gabriel proclaimed John's mission to prepare Israel for the coming of the Lord. John's first prophecy came from the womb, when his leaps identified Mary's baby as the Saviour. John (Hebrew for "God is gracious") received the name assigned by Gabriel. After preparing himself with fasting and prayer in the wilderness near the Dead Sea, John began preaching and baptizing by the Jordan River. John was no miracle worker but still people came from all over to hear his message of repentance and the coming kingdom. John had no patience for hypocrisy but gave practical commands to the sincere. Tax collectors were to take only what was due and soldiers were to stop taking bribes. John steadfastly denied he was the Messiah, saying that the one coming after him would baptize with the Holy Spirit and fire. John gathered many disciples whom he instructed in fasting and prayer, including St Andrew. John balked at baptizing his Lord when Jesus came to the Jordan River until Jesus commanded him to. After witnessing the Holy Spirit descend on Jesus, John told his disciples that Jesus was the Lamb of God. John was imprisoned in the fortress of Machaeus by Herod Antipas for publicly condemning Herod's marriage to Herodias, the wife of his half-brother. At Herod's birthday festival, Herodias's daughter danced so charmingly that Herod promised her anything. Prompted by her mother, she demanded that John be beheaded.

OTHER SAINTS • BARTHOLOMEW OF FARNE

25

WILLIAM OF MONTEVERGINE

Hermit and king's advisor b.1085, d.1142

After a pilgrimage to Compostela, Spain, William lived as a hermit on Monte Vergine, between Nola and Benevento. The disciples who followed him found his life, which included wearing mail, too strict. Not wanting to break up the community or relax his own austerities, William left with a few disciples. He continued to found monasteries until the king of Naples commanded his services as consultant. Those who envied William's influence on the king began to slander him and convinced the king to test William by sending a woman to seduce him. When the woman arrived, William parted the hearth fire with his bare hands, lay down between the embers, and invited her to share his bed. The woman was shocked to repentance and stripped off her jewellery, gave away her possessions, and entered a convent.

OTHER SAINTS • MAXIMUS OF TURIN

The arrest of John the Baptist.

26

ANTHELM
Bishop b. 1107, d. 1178

Anthelm had a lucrative church career when a visit in 1137 to the austere alpine Carthusian monastery of Portes roused a yearning for solitude. He immediately requested admission, but was never left in peace for long. After his novitiate, he repaired the buildings destroyed by an avalanche at the Grande Chartreuse monastery. Then he was appointed abbot of Portes where he distributed its wealth to the poor. He was thrust into the world again as bishop of Bellay. He enforced clerical celibacy and clashed with the local count, Humbert III, and the pope when he excommunicated the former for arresting a priest. As Anthelm lay dying from fever caught while distributing food during a famine, Humbert begged forgiveness and Anthelm blessed him.

OTHER SAINTS • SALVIUS

27

CYRIL OF ALEXANDRIA
Archbishop of Alexandria d. 444

Cyril's uncompromising stand as defender of orthodox doctrine earned him the title of Doctor of the Incarnation but also resulted in controversial acts early on in his career as archbishop of Alexandria, such as closing schismatic churches and driving the Jews out of the town. Cyril succeeded his uncle Theodosius as archbishop in 412. The legacy of Theodosius's unprincipled rule may have strengthened Cyril's resolve to base his doctrine firmly on the foundation of the church fathers. When Nestorius, a priest in Antioch, denied that Jesus was God made man, Cyril promoted orthodox doctrine through writing, appealing to the pope, and calling the council of Ephesus in 341. A rival council of Antioch bishops condemned Cyril and the emperor had both men arrested until papal legates arrived to vindicate Cyril.

OTHER SAINTS • JULIUS THE VETERAN • MELANGELL

28

IRENAEUS OF LYONS
Bishop and apologist b. 125?, d. 202?

The voice that thwarted the first great threat of heresy belonged to a bishop who lived up to his name "lover of peace." Even while defending Christianity against heresy, Irenaeus was careful to win hearts with courtesy rather than alienate with condemnation. As a Greek from Asia Minor, Irenaeus was well-educated in Greek philosophy and poetry, which gave him an excellent background for creating well-reasoned arguments for Christianity and against Gnosticism. But he received his most important education from Polycarp and others who had known the Apostles. Ireneaus went to Gaul as a missionary and was ordained in Lyons by its first bishop, Pothinus. His first mission was to plead for clemency for Montanist Christians in Rome. In his absence, Pothinus was martyred and Irenaeus was chosen to replace him. As bishop, Irenaeus sent missionaries to spread the gospel throughout Gaul and abandoned his own Greek to speak to the people in their native language. Irenaeus became more concerned about the co-opting of Christian beliefs by

"Even while defending Christianity...Irenaeus was careful to win hearts with courtesy rather than alienate with condemnation."

Gnostics. Gnosticism was difficult to define because they used secrecy to attract converts and because the doctrines were redefined by each master. Gnostics believed that God was aloof from creation and à Demiurge, or lower god (or gods), had created the world and ruled it with other spiritual beings. Irenaeus used his five volumes of *Against Heresies* to weave theological arguments and to take away some of the glamour of Gnosticism by bringing their secrets out of the shadow. Gnosticism's popularity waned in the light of his reasoning. Irenaeus prevented a schism by mediating peace between the pope and Christians in Asia Minor, who continued to use the Eastern method of calculating Easter. He pointed out that they were just following their old tradition. There is no reliable evidence of when or how Irenaeus died.

OTHER SAINTS • AUSTELL • POTAMIAENA AND BASILIDES

29

PETER

Apostle d.64?

Who would have bet the future of the church on an impulsive, uneducated fisherman who betrayed his master? But Jesus saw into Simon's heart and renamed him the "rock" (Petros in Greek). Jesus demonstrated his respect and friendship for Peter by ensuring that he accompanied him at his transfiguration and his prayer at Gethsemane. After Jesus' resurrection, Peter reconfirmed his love for Christ three times and received Jesus' mission to tend his flock. Peter, always listed as first of the Apostles, was also the first to testify on Pentecost. He left Jerusalem after escaping prison and tradition has him founding the church of Antioch. Ancient tradition says that he was killed in Rome during Nero's reign by being crucified, upside-down at his own request.

St Peter preaching in Jerusalem.

30

BERTRAND OF LE MANS

Bishop b.553?, d.623

Bertand used his authority to ensure good stewardship of the land he loved. After being ordained by St Germanus in Paris, Bertrand distinguished himself by teaching in the cathedral school and was appointed archdeacon. In 587 he was consecrated bishop of Le Mans. Perhaps his attachment to the land was deepened by the fact that political struggles resulted in his banishment from his diocese several times. He convinced local landowners to donate property to the church and then nurtured the land with wise agricultural practices. He developed the land under his control for the greater good by building religious foundations including the abbeys of Notre-Dame de la Couture and Sts Peter and Paul, as well as a hospice for travellers.

OTHER SAINTS • THEOBALD OF PROVINS • GEORGE THE HAGIORITE

1

EPARCHIUS
Monk and liberator b.509, d.581

This gentle French monk, commonly known as Cybard, opened his heart to animals and people alike. He escaped the post he held as chancellor to his uncle to retreat to the religious life. When his wisdom, and the miracles he performed, made him a celebrity he fled to the secluded, wooded loop of the river Charente. Even animals recognized his tenderness; a mother bird allowed him to lift her off her nest so he could bless her tiny fledglings. All the alms he received and most of his energy went into freeing slaves and commuting the barbaric sentences of prisoners. One document records how he purchased the freedom of 175 slaves in 1558. He was so dedicated to helping prisoners that he actually cut one man down from the gallows.

OTHER SAINTS • JULIUS AND AARON • SHENUTE • THEODORIC

2

SWITHUN OF WINCHESTER
Bishop d.862

Born in Wessex, this priest was so famous for his humble and studious nature that he was chosen by King Egbert to be his chaplain. Swithun also tutored Prince Ethelwold, who nominated Swithun to be the bishop of Winchester in 852 after he became king. He continued to have a strong moral influence on the royal line, convincing King Ethelbald to dissolve a marriage to his own stepmother. His humility extended beyond his death, as he commanded that he be buried in open ground, exposed to the careless elements and feet of travellers. Although there is no clear explanation for the legend, it was believed that if it rained on St Swithun's day, it would rain for 40 days. Some say the story was inspired by a heavy rain that fell on the date his relics were moved to the cathedral on July 15.

OTHER SAINTS • OTTO OF BAMBERG • BERNARDINO REALINO

When Thomas saw the wounds on Jesus' body, he instantly believed.

3

THOMAS
Apostle First century

Posterity has branded this Apostle "doubting Thomas" for his disbelief about the resurrection, but "believing Thomas" might better describe him since he was the first disciple to acknowledge Jesus as God. The four Gospels name Thomas as one of the 12 Apostles chosen by Jesus, with the nickname of Didymus (Greek for "twin") implying there was a now-unknown sibling. Throughout John's Gospel, Thomas's natural pragmatism is transformed by the challenge of faith. When Jesus decided to visit Judea despite plots against him, Thomas assumed the worst would happen but courageously offered to go with Jesus and die with him. Perhaps he alone believed Jesus' prophecies of his coming death. At the last supper, Thomas voiced the anguished question of how could they follow Jesus if they didn't know where he was going. Jesus responded that he was the way, the truth, and the life. After the

"...as soon as Jesus returned, the stupefied disciple forgot his need for solid proof and cried out, 'My Lord and my God'..."

resurrection, pragmatic Thomas refused to believe that the Apostles had seen Jesus, announcing that he would only be convinced by solid flesh. But as soon as Jesus returned, the stupefied disciple forgot his need for solid proof and cried out, "My Lord and my God," an affirmation of faith beyond physical evidence. What happened to Thomas after Pentecost is shrouded in legend. The historian Eusebius reports that he preached in Iran. However, there is an unshakable tradition that Thomas founded Christian communities in India, and that he was martyred and buried at Mylapore in 72AD. In 1498, the Portuguese were welcomed by Indians calling themselves the Christians of St Thomas. The four writings that have been attributed to Thomas; the Acts of Thomas, the Infancy Gospel, the Apocalypse, and the Gospel of Thomas, are all apocryphal, and are believed to have actually been written between the middle of the second and fourth centuries.

OTHER SAINTS • ANATOLIUS OF LAODICEA • HELIDORUS OF ATTINO

4

ELIZABETH OF PORTUGAL

Queen and peacemaker b.1271, d.1336

This Queen of Portugal is known as the "Peacemaker" for her success in averting war, but she also worked for peace in her own private life. Strengthened by spiritual devotion, she patiently bore the infidelities of her husband, even ensuring the welfare of his illegitimate children. But she is best remembered for her public peacemaking. She negotiated two reconciliations between her husband and their rebellious son and arranged peace between her brother, the King of Aragon, and the King of Castile. After nursing her husband through his last illness, she retired to a Franciscan tertiary. She died after one last mission to mediate between her son, by then the king, and the King of Castile.

OTHER SAINTS • BERTHA OF BLANGY • ANDREW OF CRETE

5

ANTHONY ZACCARIA

Founder of the Clerks Regular of St Paul b.1502, d.1539

In a time of religious and political unrest, Anthony was called to heal both spiritual and physical ills in the Church. As a doctor in his hometown of Cremona, Anthony realized that a true healer considered the health of the whole person. He began studying theology in order to give spiritual help as well as medical advice. After being ordained a priest, he moved to Milan where he met Bartoleomeo Ferrari and Jacobo-Antonio Morigia, who shared his desire to heal sickness in the Church. They formed the Clerks Regular of St Paul, dedicated to reforming clergy and lay people through preaching, the celebration of the sacraments, and the examples of their lives. Anthony recognized the healing power in group support and organized spiritual associations for lay people, married couples, and clergy.

OTHER SAINTS • ATHANASIUS OF JERUSALEM

6

MARIA GORETTI

Martyr b.1890, d.1902

Maria is held up as a model of chastity, but the most moving lesson of her life is in the heroic forgiveness that reached beyond death. Maria's life in her native Italy was never easy. After her father died, just getting enough to eat was a struggle. When she was 12, a teenage neighbour, Alexander, stabbed her when she refused to submit to his sexual advances. As she died, Maria forgave Alexander, but her death didn't end her concern for her murderer. Imprisoned for his crime and unrepentant, Alexander received a dream in which Maria appeared, changing his life. When he was released after 27 years, he begged and received forgiveness from Maria's mother. Alexander was in the crowd at St Peter's when Maria was canonized in 1950.

OTHER SAINTS • SISOES • PALLASIUS • SEXBURGA • GODELEVA

7

WILLIBALD OF EICHSTADT

Bishop and pilgrim b.700?, d.786?

Willibald of Eichstadt should properly be called Willibald of the World. When he was 18, his restless urge to see the world instigated a pilgrimage to Rome with his father, St Richard of the West Saxons, brother St Wunibald, and sister St Walburga. Willibald went on to physically retrace Scriptural events in the Middle East and church history in Turkey and Italy, living in fields, monasteries, and a cathedral, enduring temporary blindness and accusations of spying. When he described his adventures to Pope Gregory III in Rome, the pope realized he had found an ideal missionary to help Boniface evangelize the Germans. As bishop of Eichstadt, Willibald helped establish Christianity by supporting missionaries and founding churches and monasteries. Later, Willibald was joined in Germany by his brother and sister.

OTHER SAINTS • PANTAENUS • FELIX OF NANTES • HEDDA

Elizabeth of Portugal curing lepers.

8

GRIMBALD OF WINCHESTER

Monk and scholar b. 825?, d. 901

Rebuilding after war can involve repairing buildings, replanting crops, and rehabilitating the wounded but, after the Danish invasions ended, King Alfred of England realized that the foundation of his country's future lay in restoring its knowledge. He asked the renowned French scholar Grimbald to abandon his position at the monastery of Reims to lead the reconstruction of a strange raw land with an unknown culture and tongue. The chance to learn as well as teach must have appealed to the 60-year-old priest, for Grimbald arrived in England in 886 and never returned home. After learning the language, he renewed English scholarship by translating Latin texts into Anglo-Saxon, serving as Professor of Divinity at Oxford, and expanding England's libraries.

OTHER SAINTS • AQUILA AND PRISCA • PROCOPIUS • DISIBOD

9

VERONICA GIULIANI

Abbess b. 1660, d. 1727

An ecstatic mystic who was also a skilled administrator, Veronica didn't submit to easy labels. Her spirituality was focused on the passion of Jesus and in 1697 the physical wounds of Christ, or stigmata, appeared on her body. Though she tried to hide the wounds, the local bishop found out and had her isolated from her community and watched day and night to expose any fraud. Not only did she retain the stigmata under this degrading scrutiny but she kept her patience and humility as well. Her own community respected her common sense and not only made her novice mistress for 34 years, but elected her abbess for 11 years until her death. As abbess, she organized the finances of the community, directed construction projects, and initiated modern improvements such as a new water system.

OTHER SAINTS • AGILOLF • JOAN OF REGGIO • MARTYRS OF ORANGE

Benedict helped out a fellow monk by miraculously retrieving the head of his hedgehook when it dropped in a lake.

10

ANTONY OF THE CAVES OF KIEV

Abbot b. 983, d. 1073

Because early Russian monasteries were founded by foreigners unconnected to Russian spirituality, Antony travelled to Mount Athos in Greece to learn religious life. But, after several years, the abbot forced him to return to Russia, commanding him to use his training to teach others. Since the situation at home had not improved, Antony could only find the life he desired as a hermit in a cave in Kiev. His austere life soon attracted disciples and Antony accepted anyone who was sincere. The indigenous monastery spread from caves to buildings and its spirit spread throughout Russia. Antony succeeded where others had failed because, as his chronicler says, rather than building monasteries with wealth, Antony built his with fasting, tears, and prayer.

OTHER SAINTS • VICTORIA AND ANATOLIA • AMALBURGA

11

BENEDICT

Abbot and founder b. 480?, d. 550?

The education Benedict received in Rome was not what his parents had intended. Horrified by the emptiness of his studies and the vices of his classmates, Benedict fled to the mountains of Subiaco where he lived as a hermit. Twenty-five years later he formed a new monastic community at Monte Cassino under the rule that became the foundation of the church's monastic system, centred on Benedict's three tenets of "work, pray, read." Manual labour was necessary for the health of both body and soul. Benedict chose for his prayer the Psalms that Jesus himself had prayed. What became known as the Divine Office was so important that he called it the "Work of God." Reading consisted of *lectio divina*, sacred reading in which the words of Scripture were contemplated until they soaked into the reader's very being.

OTHER SAINTS • PIUS I • DROSTAN • JOHN OF BERGAMO • HIDULF

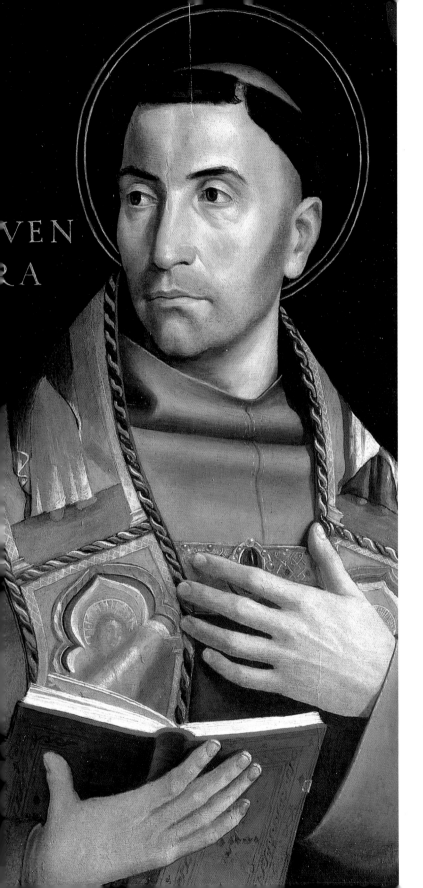

—✦ 12 ✦—

JOHN GUALBERT
Abbot and founder b.990?, d.1073

Sent by his father to avenge a relative's death, John cornered the murderer in Florence when the man spread his arms in the form of a cross and begged John to spare him for Jesus' sake. Suddenly realizing with horror what he been about to do, John dropped his sword and begged the man's forgiveness. He immediately ran to the nearby monastery of San Miniato where he dedicated his life to God. Seeking a stricter life, he left to found his own monastery at Valumbrosa, a community of hermits living under the Appenine pines. John was soon called to found other monasteries and restore discipline to others. Passionate about church reform, John tried to force the deposition of a bishop accused of simony and preached against clerical marriage.

OTHER SAINTS ✦ JOHN THE IBERIAN ✦ JOHN JONES

—✦ 13 ✦—

EUGENIUS OF CARTHAGE
Bishop d.505

Persecution by Arian Vandals prevented Catholics from filling the Carthage See for 24 years until the Vandal King allowed the consecration of Eugenius as bishop. But Eugenius's preaching attracted so many Vandals that Huneric's tolerance ended abruptly. He arrested and tortured any Vandals entering Eugenius's church. After an inconclusive peace conference between Catholic and Arian bishops, Huneric drove the Catholic bishops out of the city, trampling them with his horses. He banished those, including Eugenius, who refused to swear loyalty to his son. From Corsica, where he was sentenced to build ships, Eugenius wrote to his flock to remain steadfast. During the years that followed Huneric's death, Eugenius was restored as bishop of Carthage in 488 but five years was later banished again to Provence, where he died.

OTHER SAINTS ✦ HENRY II ✦ SILAS ✦ MILDRED

St Bonaventure combined orthodoxy with scholarship when leading the Franciscans.

— 14 —

CAMILLUS DE LELLIS

Founder of the Ministers of the Sick and patron of nurses b.1550, d.1614

Camillus lost everything to his gambling addiction and the erstwhile soldier was forced to beg for food. When Camillus found a job with masons working at a Capuchin monastery, one of the friars convinced him to change his life. An ulcerous leg, however, prevented Camillus from joining the Capuchins. He began to minister in hospitals where he was horrified at the lack of care and compassion shown to the patients. After ordination as a priest, he established the Ministers of the Sick, whose members wore a red cross on their habits. Camillus was committed to employing both classic charity and modern technology, treating his patients with enlightened methods of nutrition, quarantine, and hygiene as well as with selfless compassion.

OTHER SAINTS • DEUSDEDIT • VINCENT MADELGARIUS

— 15 —

BONAVENTURE

Cardinal, bishop, and Doctor of the Church b.1221, d.1274

Bonaventure's name means "good fortune," and certainly the church can be very thankful for the good fortune, and God's blessing, that brought Bonaventure forward at a crucial point in history. After joining the Franciscans in his native Tuscany when he was 21, Bonaventure was sent to the University of Paris where the Dominicans and Franciscans were struggling with the secular clergy for control of the education centre, each accusing the other of heresy. His reputation for orthodoxy combined with scholarship not only won him leadership of the Franciscan school but also respect from those who stereotyped Franciscans as ignorant or heretical. As general of the Franciscan Order, Bonaventure earned the appellation of Second Founder of the Franciscans because his devotion, intelligence, and innovation without

sacrificing tradition saved the Franciscans from threats that Francis never foresaw. Bonaventure conquered the difficult balancing acts of preserving the true spirit of the Franciscans but introducing vital new conditions. His austere life served as an example and curbed abuses of luxury and greed while discouraging extremist views that Franciscans should own no property. He supported the presence of Franciscans in education since people would not be converted by ignorant preachers. Bonaventure's great body of work includes treaties on theology and philosophy, Scripture commentaries, and even poetry and hymns. Throughout all his work runs a deep sense of mysticism; his belief that the purpose of human beings is to seek perfect union with God. When Pope Gregory X ordered Bonaventure to accept promotion to cardinal, the two nuncios who delivered his cardinal's mitre found him washing dinner dishes. He told them to hang the hat on a tree until he was done.

OTHER SAINTS • FELIX OF THIBIUCA • JAMES OF NISIBIS

— 16 —

MARY-MAGDALEN POSTEL

Founder of the Sisters of Mary-Magdalen Postel b.1756, d.1846

Julie Postel risked her life to maintain a hidden chapel in her house during the French Revolution. Taking risks was nothing new to the young woman who had opened her own school for girls when she was only 18. At 49, she started a new religious congregation of teachers in Cherbourg and took the name of Mary-Magdalen. After an early success, her new community was evicted for political reasons. During the years that followed, the fledgling congregation endured poverty and hardship, and even their supporters told them to give up. But for Mary-Magdalen standing fast was not a matter of risk but trust in God's plan. By the time she died, she saw her initial three teachers grow into the 150 Sisters of Christian Schools of Mercy (now the Sisters of Mary-Magdalen Postel) in 37 houses.

OTHER SAINTS • ATHENOGENES • REINELDIS • FULRAD

17

JUSTA AND RUFINA

Martyrs and patrons of Seville and potters d.287?

The historical reality of these popular Spanish martyrs is supported by evidence of their early veneration. These two women (sometimes described as sisters) sold ceramic pots in Seville. Because they were Christians, they refused to sell their merchandise for use in pagan rituals. An angry mob, formed from the rebuffed customers, smashed their pottery. When they, in turn, shattered pagan idols carried by the mob, they were denounced as Christians and arrested. They were then tortured on the rack and torn with iron hooks. Though an idol had been placed close to the rack, they refused to burn incense to it to escape their torment. Justa died of the torture but Rufina was strangled. Some accounts actually describe Justa as a man named Justus.

OTHER SAINTS • SPERATUS AND COMPANIONS • LEO IV

18

PAMBO

Founder and desert father b.303?, d.390

This Egyptian hermit, known today as one of the desert fathers and a founder of the Nitrian monasteries in lower Egypt, was renowned for his austere life, his love of silence, and his wisdom when he did choose to speak. It's reported that Pambo wanted to learn to read in order to study Scripture better. His teacher's first lesson began with the first verse of Psalm 39, which exhorts the guarding of one's mouth to prevent sinning with words. Pambo immediately announced that that was enough for one lesson, left, and didn't return for six months. When his teacher criticized him for not keeping up his lessons, Pambo answered that he hadn't perfected that one verse yet. When asked about the verse later in his life he said that after 19 years, he was still trying to master it.

OTHER SAINTS • ARNULF OF METZ • FREDERICK OF UTRECHT

Justa and Rufina are now known as the patrons of Seville and potters.

19

ARSENIUS THE GREAT

Monk b.350?, d.440

"Father of the Emperors" seems like a glorious title but Egyptian monks used it to shame Arsenius, who fled to the desert after serving as imperial tutor to the princes Honorius and Arcadius. His former pupils almost destroyed the empire with their foolishness, cruelty, and feuding. He reportedly wept so continually over his sins and responsibility in the fate of his students that he wore off his eyelashes. St John of Kolobos, doubting that Arsenius was sincere about being a monk, first ignored him and then threw a crust on the floor for him. When Arsenius sat on the floor to eat, John accepted him at Skete. Arsenius was known for his silence, saying that he always regretted his words when he spoke, but was never sorry when he kept quiet.

OTHER SAINTS • MACRINA THE YOUNGER • BERNULF OF UTRECHT

20

FRUMENTIUS

Bishop and Apostle of the Ethiopians d.380?

Remembered as Aba salama ("Father of Peace") in Ethiopia, Frumentius, a Tyrean student, initially arrived in an Ethopian port after an educational trip ended tragically with the massacre of the crew of his ship and his mentor. He and his fellow student Adensius became slaves of the king, where they served so conscientiously that the queen freed them when her husband died. At her request, they stayed to help administer the kingdom until her son was older. Frumentius encouraged Christianity, relaxing laws against Christian worship and supporting Christian settlement. After the young king took power, St Athanasius consecrated Frumentius bishop of the kingdom. Frumentius earned the appellation Apostle of the Ethiopians by preaching and converting many with the example of his holy life.

OTHER SAINTS • JOSEPH BARSABBAS • AURELIUS OF CARTHAGE

⟢ 21 ⟐

LAWRENCE OF BRINDISI
Capuchin and Doctor of the Church b.1559, d.1619

This Capuchin friar from Naples considered his talent for languages a gift from God to be used in His service. His fluency in Hebrew and Greek contributed to biblical scholarship and a papal mission for the conversion of Jews. Alongside his diplomatic skill and a reputation for holiness, his knowledge of languages took him to Germany, where he founded Capuchin friaries, nursed plague victims, and raised a German army to help the Hungarians repel the Turks. After many years of diplomatic and religious missions he retired in 1618, but was called for one last assignment – to convince the King of Spain to recall the tyrannical governor of Naples. The arduous journey hastened his death.

OTHER SAINTS • VICTOR OF MARSEILLES • ARBOGAST

⟢ 22 ⟐

MARY MAGDALEN
Disciple and first witness to the resurrection First Century

"I have seen the Lord." With these words Mary Magdalen proclaimed the miracle of the resurrection of Jesus to the disciples. Why did Christ choose to appear to Mary Magdalen first out of all his apostles? Scripture gives us a possible reason in its portrait of Mary Magdalen as a loyal disciple who stayed with Jesus when all others had deserted him. Mary probably received her name from Magdala, presumably her native town, on the western shore of the sea of Galilee. The Gospels tell us that after Jesus freed Mary from possession by seven demons, she joined other women disciples who followed Jesus in his journeys to care for him and learn from him. After Jesus' arrest, the Apostles scattered in fear, but Mary stood faithfully with his mother and John beneath the cross. Devoted to Jesus even after death, Mary watched as Jesus was buried. While the other disciples shivered in fear in a locked room, she returned to the tomb to anoint Jesus' body. It was then that she discovered the empty tomb. John tells that Mary's eyes were so filled with tears at this loss that she didn't recognize Jesus until he called her name. Then Jesus assigned her the vital mission to spread the good news of his resurrection. Popular tradition has identified her at times with Mary of Bethany and the sinner who washed Jesus' feet, which led to legends that she was a prostitute. Both these associations seem unlikely. There are many legends about what happened to Mary Magdalen after Pentecost. Eastern tradition says she lived in Ephesus with Jesus' mother, Mary, and John. Western legends relate that she evangelized France and lived in a cave in the Alps. Whatever happened, we can be certain that this devoted disciple courageously continued to spread the word that she had seen the risen Lord.

OTHER SAINTS • WANDREGISILUS • PHILIP EVANS AND JOHN LLOYD

⟢ 23 ⟐

BRIDGET OF SWEDEN
Mother, visionary, and founder b.1302, d.1373

Though Bridget led a life of holiness characterized by charity so generous that she risked prison from debts incurred in almsgiving, she is still best remembered for her visions. Whether serving God as wife and mother of eight children, including St Catherine, as the founder of the Brigettine Order, or as a pilgrim in Rome, her revelations fuelled her reforming zeal. The messages she relayed from God ranged from down-to-earth advice that Christians should bathe for health, to political pronouncements that prophesied tragedy for England if it did not make peace with France. She courageously confronted kings, bishops, and popes if her visions led her to believe that her message was necessary for their salvation or the salvation of God's people.

OTHER SAINTS • APOLLINARIS OF RAVENNA • JOHN CASSIAN

Mary Magdalen was a loyal follower of Christ.

24

BORIS AND GLEB

Martyrs of non-violence d. 1015

These two princes are venerated as martyrs in Russia because their non-violent acceptance of an unjust fate mirrored Christ's passion. Boris and Gleb (also known by their baptismal names of Romanus and David) were sons of St Vladimir of Kiev, a ruler venerated for his establishment of Christianity in Russia. Vladimir's eldest son, Svjatopolk, seized power after his father's death and plotted to rid himself of any possible rivals, including his brothers. Boris was murdered while camping with his troops, reportedly refusing to fight back out of respect for his brother's authority. Gleb was pre-warned, but an injury in a fall prevented his escape. Legend says that Gleb thanked God for letting him die before he could succumb to the temptations of the world.

OTHER SAINTS · DECLAN · JOHN BOSTE

25

CHRISTOPHER

Martyr and patron of motorists and travellers Third century?

All that is known about this popular saint is that a martyr named Christopher died for the faith in the early years of Christianity. Tradition says that Christopher was beheaded after being burned and pierced by arrows during the persecution of Emperor Decius. His reputation as patron of motorists and travellers arose from the medieval legend derived from the meaning of his name, "Christ-bearer." In this legend, he served travellers by bearing them across a dangerous river. One day he carried a child across whose weight made Christopher stagger. The child revealed himself to be Christ, burdened with the world. Since the 1969 reform of the Catholic calendar, his feast is no longer celebrated universally because of the lack of historical evidence of his life, but it may still be observed by individuals.

OTHER SAINTS · JAMES THE GREATER · THEA · OLYMPIAS

Boris and Gleb accepted their premature deaths with dignity.

26

BARTOLOMEA CAPITANIO

Founder of the Sisters of Charity of Lovere b. 1807, d. 1833

Bartolomea's boundless energy pushed her past obstacles that included her youth, her own parents, and her illness to achieve her dreams in a very short life. When her alcoholic father and pious mother refused to let her become a nun, the young Bartolomea pursued her dream to minister to young people with a private vow and a teacher's diploma. After founding youth fellowship groups, she joined forces with St Vincentia Gerosa, a woman 20 years older who had organized a hospital, to establish the Sisters of Charity of Lovere devoted to education and nursing. Though she died from tuberculosis less than a year later, Bartolomea's energy still infused the dream and the Order grew to over 8000 members in countries all over the world.

OTHER SAINTS · JOACHIM AND ANNE

27

PANTALEON

Martyr d. 305?

Though we have no historical facts about Pantaleon's life, ancient churches dedicated to him in Constantinople point to an early veneration of a martyr who died in Nicodemia during the persecution of Diocletian. Legends say that Pantaleon (or possibly Pateleimon – "All Compassionate") was the physician of Emperor Galerius Maximian. The son of a Christian mother and a pagan father, he had fallen away from his childhood faith only to be re-converted by a priest named Hermolaus. Jealous of his intimacy with the emperor, other physicians betrayed his Christianity. Pantaleon refused to deny his faith, but even when he healed a man of paralysis his accusers refused to believe the truth and he was beheaded. In the East he is venerated as one of the Holy Moneyless saints because he treated the sick for free.

OTHER SAINTS · CELESTINE I · AURELIUS · RAYMUND PALMARIUS

28

SAMSON OF BRITTANY
Bishop d.565?

When this Welsh monk heard that his dying father was asking for him, he refused to go back into the world until his abbot, Piro, commanded him. Samson's father, Amwyn, was healed by his son's administration of the Sacraments and consecrated his life to God, accompanying Samson on his travels. Samson's election as abbot after Piro's death was short-lived because his monks did not like his reforms. When Samson received a vision commanding him to go to Brittany as a missionary, he set sail with Amwyn. After landing, he hitched up a cart purchased in Ireland, filled it with books and vestments, and set out. He founded churches in Golant and Southill and two monasteries, including one at Dol where he settled and became bishop.

OTHER SAINTS • VICTOR I • MELCHIOR GARCÍA SAMPREDRO

29

MARTHA
Disciple First century

John's Gospel explicitly states that Jesus loved Martha, her sister Mary, and her brother Lazarus. Jesus was a frequent visitor to Martha's home in Bethany, a small village two miles from Jerusalem, where Martha took pleasure in serving him. Concerned with hospitality, during one visit she became frustrated when her sister Mary didn't help her serve Jesus and the disciples. Jesus lovingly observed her anxiety and reminded her that only one thing was important – being with him. Martha showed the depth of her faith when, grieving over the death of Lazarus, she proclaimed her belief in Jesus' power, in the resurrection, and that Jesus was the Son of God, whereupon Jesus restored her brother to life. According to an untrustworthy legend, Martha accompanied Mary Magdalen to evangelize France after Pentecost.

OTHER SAINTS • LUPUS OF TROYES • WILLIAM OF SAINT-BRIEUC

30

PETER CHRYSOLOGUS
Bishop and Doctor of the Church b.380?, d.449?

The name of this Doctor of the Church translates to "Golden Words" or "Golden Speaker," reflecting his reputation for persuasive preaching as bishop of Ravenna. Seventy-six of his sermons still exist. Their subject matter, on Scripture and the reformation of life, was timeless and their brevity showed Peter's instinctive understanding of his hearers' attention spans. Nevertheless, the written words fail to convey through the centuries the fervour and enthusiasm that often overwhelmed him to the point of speechlessness. In his own diocese he worked hard to eradicate vestiges of paganism among the people and backed the doctrine of the incarnation against those who doubted Christ's divinity, saying that divisions in the church caused grief in heaven.

OTHER SAINTS • JULITTA • LEOPOLD MANDIC

31

IGNATIUS OF LOYOLA
Founder of the Society of Jesus b.1491, d.1556

While recovering from a battle wound, this soldier discovered a glory greater than military success within a book on the saints' lives. Retreating to a cave to seek God's will, he developed a process of discernment and meditation using the senses and the imagination, which he later developed into the classic "Spiritual Exercises." After being investigated by the Inquisition, he realized education would increase the credibility of his teachings so he went back to school. In Paris, he gathered six followers who became the core of the Society of Jesus, or Jesuits. Whether founding universities or evangelizing foreign lands, this soldier of God insisted that the direction of the society come from prayer. By the time of his death, the Jesuits had grown to 1500 members with 35 colleges and houses in 11 countries.

OTHER SAINTS • GERMANUS OF AUXERRE • HELEN OF SKÖVDE

Ignatius performing miracles in front of the people.

CURE of ARS

1

ALPHONSUS LIGUORI

Bishop, founder of the Redemptorists, and Doctor of the Church b.1696, d.1787

Alphonsus was a successful Neapolitan lawyer when bribery in court made him rethink the value of worldly success and devote his life to God. Through a hatred of idleness, he drove himself so hard in ministry that he had a breakdown. While recovering in the mountains of Scala, he discovered people neglected by the church and ignorant of faith. After one unsuccessful attempt, he founded the Congregation of the Most Holy Redeemer, or Redemptorists, dedicated to serving the poor and most abandoned. A groundbreaking theologian, Alphonsus was appointed bishop of Sant' Agata against his will, where he worked hard to alleviate the physical and spiritual ills of his people, while suffering himself from a permanently bent neck.

OTHER SAINTS • EXSUPERIUS • ALED • ETHELWOLD

2

EUSEBIUS OF VERCELLI

Bishop d.371

Eusebius learned how to persevere as a Christian from his father, who died a martyr in Sardinia. After being elected bishop by the people and clergy of Vercelli, Eusebius was sent to a council convened by Emperor Constantius in 355, supposedly to work out disagreements between Arians and Catholics. When the Arians turned the peace council into a condemnation of St Athanasius, their chief opponent, Eusebius, courageously demanded that everyone sign the Nicene Creed, proclaiming Jesus to be one with the Father, a belief Arians opposed. The result was his exile to Scythopolis, where Arians harassed him by beatings, imprisonments, and even ransacked his house. Constantius's successor, Julian, revoked the banishment, and Eusebius took the long way home so he could preach throughout the empire.

OTHER SAINTS • RUTILIUS • SYAGRIUS • THOMAS OF DOVER

John Vianney wore himself out listening to the confessions of ordinary people.

3

LYDIA

Early convert of St Paul First century

Everything we know about the first European convert of St Paul comes from Luke's account in the Acts of the Apostles. After Paul and his missionaries arrived in the Roman colony of Philippi, they went to synagogue on the Sabbath and began to instruct some women they found gathered there. One of the women was Lydia, a dealer in purple cloth from the city of Thyatira, in what is now western Turkey. Described as a "God-fearer," someone attracted to Judaism without having fully converted, she heard the truth in Paul's preaching and was baptized with her household. She insisted that Paul and his missionaries accept the hospitality of her home if he found her faithful to the Lord and she also sheltered them after they were attacked and arrested.

OTHER SAINTS • ASPRENATIS OF NAPLES • MARTIN OF CAMPANIA

4

JOHN VIANNEY

Patron of parish priests and curé of Ars b.1786, d.1859

There was only one thing to do with a priest like John who, despite tutoring and cramming, had flunked his seminary classes – he was assigned to the remote rural parish of Ars where he could do the least harm. But the parishioners became fascinated with the new priest because he prayed all night and gave his clothes to beggars. He may not have understood Latin but he understood people, helping shopkeepers with bookkeeping and prescribing remedies for whooping cough. But it was his reputation as a confessor who could to see into souls that brought thousands of pilgrims from all over Europe to the tiny town. He wore himself out spending 17 hours a day in the confessional. The priest that no one had wanted became the patron saint of parish priests.

OTHER SAINTS • ELEUTHERIUS OF TARSUS • IA • MOLUA

5

OSWALD
King and martyr b.604, d.642

The king who took Christianity to Northern England was a frightened little boy in 616, escaping to Scotland after his uncle had overthrown his father. The compassion of the Christian Scots who sheltered him converted him. When Oswald reconquered Northumbria from the Britons in 633, he took his new faith with him. He then used his power to unite his territory and to spread the Gospel. His former hosts sent St Aidan and other missionaries at his appeal. He humbly translated Aidan's sermons until the Scottish saint could learn the language. Oswald was killed defending his land against the pagan Mercians and his last words were reportedly a prayer for his enemies, "My God, save their souls."

OTHER SAINTS • ADDAI AND MARI • MARGARET THE BAREFOOTED

6

JUSTUS AND PASTOR
Martyrs and patrons of Madrid and Alcalá d.304?

Though the veneration of these popular Spanish martyrs is ancient, the details of their lives are lost. Dacian, the governor of Spain, took the imperial edicts against Christians as a personal charge and travelled through his province to exterminate the faith. When he arrived in Alcalá, two brothers, aged thirteen and nine, decided to witness for their faith like the martyrs, and left school to seek out Dacian. When the boys found Dacian interrogating Christians, they drew attention by reciting the creed and other professions of faith. Dacian thought he could whip them into better behaviour, but not only did they remain steadfast, they encouraged each other. So impressive was their example to the crowd, that Dacian had them executed secretly to prevent any further conversions that their courage might inspire.

OTHER SAINTS • HORMISDAS

7

CAJETAN
Founder of the Theatines Clerks Regular b.1480, d.1547

In the 1500s, the church was in sad shape. People could not get the spiritual nourishment they needed from the uneducated and even immoral priests who took their money but gave nothing in return – and the hierarchy seemed indifferent to these ills. What could one man do? After being ordained in 1516, Cajetan established religious associations known as oratories for the clergy in his hometown of Vincenza and Verona to promote spiritual life and care for the poor and sick. He told the priests in his communities that, though they tried to serve God through worship, they would actually find Him in the hospital where they nursed patients with incurable diseases. But even close contact with suffering and disfigurement didn't horrify Cajetan as much as the greed and sinfulness he saw among many of the clergy. In 1523, he returned to Rome, not to present his concerns to church hierarchy but to consult with

"He told the priests in his communities that, though they tried to serve God through worship, they would actually find Him in the hospital where they nursed patients with incurable diseases."

a religious association called the Oratory of the Divine Love that he had joined when studying for the priesthood. There he found other concerned clergy who wanted to restore the church. They all agreed to focus on moral lives, sacred studies, preaching and pastoral care, service to the needy, and other solid foundations of pastoral life, hoping their example would inspire other clergy to reform. The Theatines Clerks Regular, so-called because it was an Order of the regular clergy and because Bishop Theatensis was their first superior general, persevered despite hostility from the very clergy they hoped to inspire. During his final illness, his doctors tried to move Cajetan from the boards he slept on to a mattress, but Cajetan said that since his saviour had died on a cross, they should at least allow him to die on wood.

OTHER SAINTS • SIXTUS AND COMPANIONS • AFRA • VICTRICIUS

Catejan worked hard to reform the church.

8

DOMINIC

Founder of the Order of Preachers (Dominicans) b.1170?, d.1221

Dominic, a Spanish priest, and his friend Bishop Diego de Azevado of Osma were horrified at the spread of heresy they discovered on a journey to Germany. Their debates with the Cathars, who believed in two gods, one good and one evil, fuelled them with zeal for missionary work. Dominic gained converts through his joyful attitude as well as his debating skill. He decried violence, saying that people should arm themselves with prayer, not swords, to fight heresy. After Diego's death, Dominic formed the first community of preachers in 1216 in Toulouse. Dominic split it up for safety when Toulouse was attacked and sent groups of two to four preachers out through Europe – the first steps towards the worldwide Order of Preachers.

OTHER SAINTS • CYRIACUS AND COMPANIONS • FAMIAN

9

TERESA BENEDICTA OF THE CROSS

Also known as Edith Stein, Carmelite nun and martyr b.1891, d.1941

An insatiable thirst for truth led this German daughter of a devout Jewish family to philosophy. But the peace of a widowed Christian friend made Edith realize that faith might be a surer road to truth. Edith became a renowned lecturer and writer in Catholic philosophy, especially women's issues, until Nazis forced her from her university position because of her background. This loss gave her the opportunity to live a contemplative life and she joined the Carmelites, becoming Teresa Benedicta of the Cross. When Germany invaded Holland, where she had been sent for safety, its bishops protested German treatment of Jews. Germany retaliated, arresting Catholics of Jewish origin. Edith was sent to Auschwitz where she died in the gas chamber.

OTHER SAINTS • ROMANUS • MIRO • NATHY AND FELIM

Clare knew from a young age that she was called to a holy life.

10

LAWRENCE

Deacon and martyr d.258

Though all that is known for certain about Lawrence is that he served as archdeacon under Pope St Sixtus and was martyred four days after his pope was, the traditional stories of his passion reflect a sense of humour in adversity. After the pope's execution, the prefect told Lawrence there would be no more persecution if he would surrender the valuables of the church to the emperor. Lawrence returned with a crowd of widows, orphans, poor, blind, and disabled people, and declared that these were the treasure of the church. Furious, the prefect condemned Lawrence to be burned to death on a blazing gridiron. Lawrence bore this torture with patient good humour, telling his executioners to turn him over because he was done on one side.

OTHER SAINTS • AUCTORIS OF METZ • ARIGIUS OF LYONS

11

CLARE OF ASSISI

Founder of the Poor Clares and patron of television b.1194, d.1253

This strong-willed 18-year-old was so moved by the preaching of Francis of Assisi that she begged him to receive her into a life of holy poverty dedicated to God. Though her family at first tried to drag her back, her conviction eventually persuaded her sisters and mother to join her in a new contemplative order subsisting solely on alms. She was the first woman to write a rule governing a convent and she was steadfast in affirming her direction in the face of opposition by authorities including the pope, who wanted to moderate their poverty. To him she replied that she needed to be absolved from her sins, not from following Jesus. Pius XII named her the patron of television in 1958 because, when illness kept her bedridden, she heard and saw the Mass from her bed as if she were there.

OTHER SAINTS • ALEXANDER THE CHARCOAL BURNER • RUSTICOLA

12

EUPLIUS

Deacon and martyr for the Gospel d. 304

Euplius was arrested for the crime of reading the Gospel, which had been banned by the emperor. When the governor of Catana commanded him to read from the forbidden book, Euplius selected Jesus' promise to those who were persecuted for righteousness and his exhortation to his followers to take up the cross. When the governor demanded an explanation of these passages, Euplius replied that they were the law of his Lord. After three months of imprisonment, Euplius was asked if he still had the illegal writings and where they were. He pointed to his heart and said, "Within me." He was told he would be saved if he sacrificed to their gods; he replied that he could only sacrifice himself to Jesus. He was beheaded with the Gospel hung around his neck.

OTHER SAINTS • HERCULANUS • LELIA • JAMES DOMAI NAM

13

RADEGUND

Queen and abbess b. 518, d. 587

By the age of 12, this German princess had lived as a captive of the uncle who killed her father and then of Clothaire, King of Neustria, who overthrew her uncle. After all this violence, she took happily to a quiet life as Clothaire's captive in France until he decided to marry her. In contrast to her brutish husband, Radegund devoted herself to serving the poor, even caring for lepers in a hospital she founded. Radegund bore her husband's cruelties and infidelities patiently, until he murdered her brother. She fled from him to seek the life consecrated to God that she had longed for. After a faint-hearted attempt to retrieve her, Clothaire left her in peace, and even helped to build her convent of the Holy Cross, which she turned into a centre for scholarship and study known throughout France.

OTHER SAINTS • PONTIAN • HIPPOLYTUS • BENILDUS

14

MAXIMILIAN KOLBE

Franciscan priest, publisher, and martyr b. 1894, d. 1941

Maximilian Kolbe combined a passion for modern technology with traditional devotion to combat the immorality of his times. He not only witnessed to the Gospel in his publications but, in the most personal way, lived out Jesus' statement that there is no greater love than to lay down one's life for another (Jn 15:13). Maximilian, who almost quit the seminary because he was more interested in technology than theology, was a young Polish Franciscan who believed that Mary's maternal example could teach people to be more compassionate. In 1922, he begged money to produce the first issue

"Maximilian. . .in the most personal way, lived out Jesus' statement that there is no greater love than to lay down one's life for another."

of *Knight of Mary Immaculate.* Within three years its circulation had grown to 70,000 copies. Not content with a magazine devoted to Mary, he built the self-supporting town of Mary the Immaculate (Niepoklanow), which housed over 760 inhabitants by 1939. Despite a lifelong struggle with tuberculosis that cost him one lung, he used state-of-the-art equipment to produce 11 publications as well as broadcast messages from his own radio station. Yet his messages, most of them written himself, were simple and straightforward, aimed at the ordinary Catholic, not intellectuals. When Poland was invaded by Germany, Maximilian defied German wrath by sheltering thousands of Polish refugees, including Jews. In 1941, he was sent to Auschwitz where he continued to minister in spite of the inhuman conditions. Then, in retaliation for an escape, 10 innocent men were sentenced to be starved to death. Maximilian volunteered to take the place of one of the condemned men and was placed in a bunker without food or water. Maximilian, who raised the spirits of the other prisoners by leading hymns, was finally executed by lethal injection. The man Maximilian saved survived to return to his family and to see Maximilian canonized.

OTHER SAINTS • MARCELLUS • URSICIUS • FACHANAN

◆══ 15 ══◆

MARY

Mother of Jesus Christ First century

Why did God choose Mary? Scripture reveals qualities invaluable for the mother of God's Son. Her courage helped her to face rejection for being unmarried and pregnant, to live as a refugee to Egypt, and to stand beneath the cross. Mary, as Luke tells us, wasn't quick to judge or panic but pondered ideas she didn't understand. But her most valuable virtue was her faith, first as a pious Jew who accepted God's will that she bear his Son, and later as the mother who, at the wedding at Cana, initiated her son's first miracle. Though Mary's later life is shrouded in legend, the assumption celebrates the belief that Mary, because she was preserved from sin as the mother of God, didn't die but was assumed bodily into heaven at the end of her life.

OTHER SAINTS • SIMPLICIAN • ALIPIUS • ATHANASIA • HYACINTH

◆══ 16 ══◆

ROCK

Pilgrim and healer d. 1378

Tradition states that this patrician native of Montpelier went on a pilgrimage to Italy, barefoot and wearing sackcloth, after his parents' deaths. Arriving in the middle of a plague, Rock cared for the neglected victims as he travelled, even producing cures. In Rome, he lived a life of prayer and nursed the sick while living off the alms he begged. On his way home, he succumbed to the plague himself and crawled into the forest so he wouldn't infect anyone but was saved when a dog brought help. Made unrecognizable by the travails of his journeys and illness, he was imprisoned as a spy, either in Lombardy or Montpelier. When the horrible conditions brought on his death, the ragged vagrant was identified as the pilgrim nephew of the governor of Montpelier.

OTHER SAINTS • THEODORE OF VALAIS • BEATRICE DA SILVA

The glorious assumption of Mary.

JOAN OF THE CROSS
Founder of the Sisters of St Anne b.1666, d.1736

When Joan inherited her mother's struggling shop, her business talents soon produced change – not just in the shop's finances but in Joan's spiritual well-being. To make more money she opened the shop on Sundays, rented rooms to pilgrims, and bought just enough food for each meal so she could tell beggars there was no food in the house. But as profit grew so did Joan's depression, and she became convinced that her vocation lay in building up the church not her business. Her shop became Providence House for those in need and her helpers the Sisters of St Anne. Larger houses were soon needed to shelter the growing numbers of orphans, sick, and elderly who came to the former businesswoman who had learned that her true profit lay in heaven.

OTHER SAINTS • MAMUS • CLARE OF MONTEFALCO

JOHN EUDES
Founder of Congregation of Jesus and Mary b.1601, d.1680

Though John overcame indifferent religious instruction as a child to become a priest, he believed that parish education was lacklustre and had weakened French faith. To counteract this, he preached missions throughout Normandy, sparking interest with processions, devotions, plays, and mime. When he had attracted the attention of the people, he engaged their intellect to explain the faith. He reinforced the renewal through written messages. But he knew he needed to strike at the root of the problem, ignorant clergy, so he founded the Congregation of Jesus and Mary, dedicated to educating priests. Despite opposition from both a diocese who considered clerical education their prerogative and a suspicious king, he lived to see his congregation approved.

OTHER SAINTS • MAGNUS OF FABRATERIA • POPE SIXTUS III

HELEN
Queen and pilgrim d.328?

The mother of Emperor Constantine was born in Drepanum (later Helenopolis). She married General Constantius Chlorus and bore his son in 274. After Constantius became Caesar, he divorced Helen to make a political marriage though Constantine still succeeded his father upon his death. After her son's conversion to Christianity in 312, Helen also embraced the faith at the age of 64. When she was about 77, she took a pilgrimage to Palestine where she remained until her death, living in a convent and performing household chores while she built shrines and basilicas in Bethlehem and on the Mount of Olives. She helped prisoners, the poor, orphans, and monasteries. The tradition that she found the true Cross is not recorded by any contemporary Christian historians.

OTHER SAINTS • AGAPITUS • MACARIUS THE WONDER WORKER

Sts Helen and Herachius take the Cross to Jerusalem.

BERNARD OF CLAIRVAUX
Doctor Mellifluous, abbot of Clairvaux, and Cistercian monk b.1091, d.1153

Bernard showed up at the Citeaux monastery not alone, but leading 31 other nobles whom he had persuaded to become Cistercian monks with him. Bernard used charisma, intelligence, and conviction to lead others in causes he considered just, ranging from faith to architecture. Though he sought peace in the monastery of Clairvaux that he had founded near a clear stream in deep woods, he was so outspoken he could never be a private figure. The French king and bishops bowed to his decision between two rival popes. Thousands answered his call to a second crusade. He believed God should be experienced rather than rationalized and fought against intellectualization of faith. His commitment to what was right was sometimes expressed in harsh judgements but he was compassionate to all those who sought his help.

OTHER SAINTS • PHILIBERT • LEOVIGILD AND CHRISTOPHER

21

PIUS X
Pope b.1835, d.1914

Giuseppe Mechior Sarto came from an Italian family so poor that he carried his shoes on the long walk to school so he wouldn't wear them out. Although he rose up through the church to cardinal and patriarch of Venice he did so by serving as a pastor, specializing in instructing children, not as a politician. In 1903, he was elected pope and chose the name Pius. He saw himself as the defender and pastor of the ordinary Catholic. This role led him to label the theological research of the times as "Modernism" and repress it as poisonous to faith. But it also led the former catechist to take the revolutionary steps of lowering the age children could receive the Body of Christ, advocating frequent, even daily, communion, and daily reading of the Scripture.

OTHER SAINTS • AGATHONICUS AND COMPANIONS • BASSA

22

SYMPHORIAN
Martyr d.200?

When the pagan procession through Autun, France passed Symphorian, the young nobleman refused to genuflect to the idols as prescribed by law and was immediately carried by the offended bystanders to the governor. Symphorian replied to interrogation that he was a Christian and refused to adore idols. He defiantly asked for a hammer so he could show the proper respect to the gods. The governor told Symphorian his rank would not protect him and ordered him to be beaten and imprisoned. When Symphorian refused the bribe of military appointment in return for honouring gods, he was condemned. As he was escorted to his execution, his mother stood on the walls of the city and shouted to him to remember the living God and not to fear the death that leads to eternal life.

OTHER SAINTS • ANTHUSA AT TARSUS • SIGRID • PHILIP BENIZI

23

ROSE OF LIMA
Lay Dominican and patroness of Central and South America b.1586, d.1617

Though Rose was the first person born in the Americas to be canonized, much of her spirituality is disturbing to modern hearts. But within her excesses is a core message of a strong young woman who fought to focus her life on the love of God despite the pressure of relatives, friends, and her own emotional problems. The young woman who struggled against the world's obsession with outward appearance earned the nickname Rose as a baby in Lima, Peru, because of her singular beauty. Fearing the temptation of vanity and attention, she filled gloves intended to soften her hands with nettles, rubbed her eyes with pepper when her mother paraded her before visitors, and destroyed her hands with lime when complimented. Though she worked long hours sewing and selling flowers to support herself and her mother, she committed her life to God, living in a shed in the garden, spending 12 hours

"Rose...fought to focus her life on the love of God despite the pressure of relatives, friends, and her own emotional problems."

a day in prayer, and joining the Third Order of the Dominicans. She stood fast in the face of insults and humiliation from those who didn't understand her, which included members of the clergy. Her spirituality centred around her simple life. She spent all of her time in communion with God, immersed in prayer and doing acts of penance, cultivating a vibrant inner spiritual life. To her it wasn't the wind that made the tree leaves clap or poplars bow down, rather it was their response to her exhortation to praise God. Filled with joy, she traded spontaneous verses with a singing bird for an hour. Though her family and clergy looked on her without comprehension, the people of Lima loved their Rose, who turned her family house into an infirmary for the poor where she nursed and sheltered many of the sick. Her funeral was delayed for days because of the crowds that filled the streets towards the cemetery, hoping for one last look at their little saint.

OTHER SAINTS • CLAUDIUS • LUPPUS • EUGENE OF ARDSTRAW

Rose cared for the sick in her own home.

24

BARTHOLOMEW
Apostle First century

Bartholomew is one of the 12 Apostles named in the Gospels of Matthew, Mark, and Luke, though no further information is given about him. Some scholars identify Bartholomew with Nathanael, the Israelite evangelized by Philip in the Gospel of John. "Bartholomew," which means "son of Tolmai," could be describing Nathanael's parentage. Though "Tolmai" probably refers to the king whose daughter married King David, St Jerome interpreted "Tolmai" as "Ptolemy," making him of royal Egyptian descent. The most trustworthy tradition reports that Bartholemew travelled to Syria with Philip after Pentecost and then preached throughout Armenia after Philip's death, until he reached Derbend where he was flayed alive and beheaded.

OTHER SAINTS • JOAN ANTIDE-THOURET • EMILY DE VIALAR

25

JOSEPH CALASANCZ
Founder of the Clerks Regular of the Religious Schools b.1556, d.1648

Joseph left a successful ecclesiastical career as vicar general of Urgel in Spain to follow an inner calling to teach poor children. When secular schools and religious orders lacked the resources to implement his proposals for free schools, he took on the job himself. With three other priests, he opened a free school in 1597 that had 100 pupils after its first week. His initial school expanded to 1000 pupils, other schools were opened, and his community was recognized as a religious order. But professional success led to personal humiliation, as an ambitious member, Mario Sozzi, conspired against Joseph, spreading slander, wrestling control of the Order from him, even prompting his arrest. Throughout this, Joseph remained forgiving, even sheltering one of his persecutors from attack, but didn't live to see his vindication.

OTHER SAINTS • GENESIUS OF ARLES • MENNAS • LOUIS OF FRANCE

26

MAXIMILIAN
Conscientious objector and martyr d.295

Though Christians have differed on whether Jesus' teachings allow military service, Maximilian believed as a soldier of Christ he could never be a soldier of the world. As the son of a Roman soldier he was required by Roman law to serve in the army, but, in the face of death, he repeated his belief that military service was against God's law. His father, also a Christian, refused to exhort him to do otherwise. Confronted with examples of Christians who served in the army, Maximilian replied that he couldn't speak for those others, but as a Christian he could not serve. When condemned to die, he announced he wouldn't perish because he was numbered in God's ranks. He was beheaded at the age of 21, and his father followed him soon after.

OTHER SAINTS • TARSICUS • ANASTASIUS THE FULLER • ADRIAN

27

MONICA
Mother of St Augustine of Hippo b.332?, d.387?

Monica earned the sympathy of generations of parents for her years of prayer for her unbelieving, reprobate son. Born in North Africa to a Christian family, Monica faced the trials of a childhood drinking problem and a troubled marriage to a pagan official that produced three children including Augustine, who rejected her faith and its morality. After following Augustine to Milan to try to reform him, Monica won the respect of Milan's bishop, St Ambrose, who congratulated Augustine for having such a mother. Ambrose's influence on Augustine led to his baptism. After his conversion, Augustine experienced a spiritual union with his mother deeper than their family bonds. God's fulfilment of Monica's prayers was delayed but abundant, as her erring son went on to become bishop, saint, and Doctor of the Church.

OTHER SAINTS • MARCELLUS OF TOMI AND COMPANIONS

A·U·G·U·S·T

— 28 —

AUGUSTINE OF HIPPO

Bishop and Doctor of the Church b. 354, d. 430

Though Augustine's initial surrender to Christianity was made famous by his *Confessions*, Augustine considered conversion a lifelong process. Rejecting his mother's Christian faith, young Augustine headed off to school in Carthage, where, like many young boys set free from family oversight, he indulged in any vice available. At 18, he took a mistress with whom he lived faithfully for 15 years and had a son, Theodatus, whom they both adored. But over the years he began to see his worldly dreams as empty and his heart began to yearn for something lasting. His forays into other sects and philosophies left him unsatisfied until St Ambrose of Milan convinced him of the intellectual truth of Christianity. Knowing the truth and living it were two very different

> *"He continued to influence the church with his writing...was patient with those who didn't have his learning."*

things and Augustine struggled to embrace the Christian life, knowing that it would mean giving up worldly pleasures. After his baptism, he continued his conversion in a small community in Africa where he wrote theological works so popular that a crowd in Hippo forced his ordination. Three years later he was consecrated bishop. He continued to influence the church with his writing, whether through his multi-volume *City of God* or a letter to little girl explaining the Our Father. He was patient with those who didn't have his learning, refusing to correct someone who spoke ignorantly as long as the subject wasn't on matters of faith. Though he suffered from asthma, he preached at least once a day. At a time when heresies threatened the church, he fought for Catholic unity with his words and his example, for which he was beaten and almost murdered. He refused to retaliate in kind, even saving condemned heretics from execution. His humility is revealed in his last book, *Retractions*, which points out everything he thought wrong in his earlier writings, showing his continual desire to work on his conversion.

OTHER SAINTS • HERMES • PELAGIUS • JULIAN OF BRIOUDE

St Augustine preached every single day.

29

JEANNE JUGAN

Founder of the Little Sisters of the Poor b.1792, d.1879

At 47, this Breton peasant quit her job as a maid to devote herself to the poor. When her employer asked where she would get money for this ministry, she told him, "From people like you." He was the first of many to open his purse for Jeanne. She and her two companions, one 70 and the other 17, took in homeless elderly women, giving up their own beds to their guests. By 1852, her community, Little Sisters of the Poor, served 1500 residents in 15 houses. But Jeanne herself had been forced out by the self-appointed father general of the Order who took away her duties, confined her to the convent, and finally eradicated her name from the Order's history. She remained serene through 37 years of abuse, and was only vindicated after her death.

OTHER SAINTS • PHILONIDIS • ADELF OF METZ • MEDERICUS

30

PAMMACHIUS

Founder of first hospice and husband d.410

A Roman senator and proconsul, Pammachius exchanged rank and privilege for poverty and service and, as St Jerome said, the world that ignored him when he was a rich patrician admired him as a poor monk. Pammachius became friends with St Jerome when they were students together. Jerome respected his friend's learning, describing Pammachius's zeal in studying the sacred writings as greater than his own. The often inflammatory Jerome took pains to explain his statements to Pammachius when the friends disagreed. Pammachius, for his part, tried to influence his friend to take a more moderate tone in his writings, even withdrawing one of his books from publication to prevent damage to his friend's reputation. In 385, Pammachius married Paulina, the daughter of St Paula. It must have been a successful marriage because Pammachius objected strongly to Jerome's preference of virginity over marriage. When Paulina died in childbirth 10 years later after several miscarriages, Pammachius honoured her memory by holding a feast for the poor after her funeral. The heartbroken Pammachius replaced his purple robes of rank for a monk's habit and dedicated his life to serving Christ. Jerome said that Pammachius decorated his wife's grave with almsgiving instead of the usual roses and violets. Whenever he left his home, the poor would crowd around him, knowing he would never refuse their requests. Pammachius started a hospice for strangers at the same time that St Fabiola founded a similar institution for the homeless. At first, Jerome says, the two saints competed in showing kindness until they realized that they could do more together than separately. They combined their resources to establish the first Western hospital and ministered to the destitute sick.

OTHER SAINTS • FELIX AND ADAUCTUS • MARGARET WARD

31

JOSEPH OF ARIMATHEA AND NICODEMUS

Jewish leaders and followers of Jesus First century

The Gospels describe Joseph as a wealthy but just man from Arimathea. He was a secret disciple of Jesus because of his position on the Jewish council of leaders. After Jesus' crucifixion, he courageously stepped forward to retrieve Jesus' body and buried it in his family tomb. Legends say he established the Christian community in Lydda. Medieval legends associate him with the Holy Grail, the chalice from the Last Supper. Nicodemus was a Jewish leader as well, and he also visited Jesus in secret. He was the catalyst for Jesus' famous speech on rebirth through baptism, which he struggled to understand. Nicodemus defended Jesus to the chief priests and Pharisees when they plotted against him, and bought spices to embalm Jesus' body.

OTHER SAINTS • PAULINUS OF TRIER • EANSWIDA • CUTHBURGA

St Joseph was a wealthy but courageous disciple.

1

DRITHELM
Monk d. 700?

Mourners weeping by the corpse of this Northumbrian family man fled in terror when he sat up. Drithelm told his wife that he had returned from the dead to live a much different life. He divided his goods among his family and the poor and became a monk at Melrose Abbey. To sincere seekers, he described a shining escort who had shown him the furnace of hell and the place where souls who had not repented until death were tossed from flames to ice before gaining heaven. Of heaven he saw only enough to make him long for more. When people wondered at Drithelm's practice of reciting prayers in an icy river, he simply replied, "I have seen greater cold." The holiness of his life spoke even louder than his words.

OTHER SAINTS • VERENA • SIMEON STYLITES THE ELDER • GILES

2

WILLIAM OF ROSKILDE
Bishop d. 1076

William went to Denmark as the English chaplain of King Cnut and stayed to evangelize the Danes as bishop of Rothskilde. In spite of his deep attachment to King Swend, and perhaps even inspired by his concern for the man, William confronted his friend on his unacceptable behaviour. William objected to Swend's marriage to his own stepdaughter, even requesting the pope's intervention to convince Swend to dissolve the union. When Swend ordered the murder of some men who insulted him, William barred his entrance to Mass until Swend confessed and was absolved. Their friendship actually grew stronger after these confrontations. When William saw Swend's funeral procession, he prayed he would not be separated from his best friend, then laid down on the ground, and died. They were buried side by side.

OTHER SAINTS • ANTONINUS • AGRICOLUS OF AVIGNON

Gregory the Great dictating a manuscript.

3

GREGORY THE GREAT
Pope and Doctor of the Church b. 540?, d. 604

Although the son of a senator, Gregory had no intention of being "Great." After his father's death, he distributed his inheritance to the poor and the church and became a monk. However, his retreat was constantly disturbed by popes needing his administrative expertize until he was finally elected pope himself. The only one who didn't agree with the unanimous election was Gregory. From the start he provided strong leadership, and reformed the clergy, evangelized England through St Augustine, promoted monasticism, renewed liturgy with the plainchant – the ritual chant of the early Christian church – and wrote books on Scripture, pastoral care, and saints' lives, as well as 854 letters. "Great" is too humble an adjective for what he achieved.

OTHER SAINTS • PHOEBE • MACANISIUS • REMACLUS • AIGULF

4

ROSE OF VITERBO
Prophet and patroness of Italian florists d. 1252?

The voice of Rose, an impoverished 12-year-old girl, preaching in the streets not only called her neighbours to repent but chastized them for surrendering to the invader Frederick II. A member of the Franciscan Third Order from the time she was eight, Rose attracted crowds who surrounded her family's house. When her anxious father threatened to punish her if she continued, Rose replied that if Jesus could be beaten for her, she could be beaten for him. She also attracted the negative attention of the ruling party who supported Frederick, who banished her at the age of 14. When she returned after Frederick's death, nuns at a local convent refused to accept Rose because she was too poor and then forced the closure of the community Rose tried to establish. Rose died at her family home when she was about 17.

OTHER SAINTS • MARCELLUS • MARINUS • ROSALIA OF PALERMO

— 5 —

LAWRENCE GIUSTINIANI
Patriarch of Venice b.1381, d.1455

When he was 19 years old, Lawrence had a dream of Eternal Wisdom in the form of a woman who exhorted him to look for peace inside his soul instead of outside in the world. As a result, he became a monk and struggled to learn humility, even biting his tongue when tempted to justify himself. When criticized by other monks for wearing rags, he responded that those who renounce the world should boldly seek the scorn of others. He was promoted to bishop of Venice and later patriarch, but continued to live austerely, saying that the only ornament of a bishop should be his virtue. He distributed food and clothes to the crowds of poor who begged at his home and sent women volunteers to seek out poor people that were too proud to ask for help.

OTHER SAINTS · BERTINUS

— 6 —

MAGNUS OF FÜSSEN
Missionary and monk d.772?

Sifting through the conflicting stories of this popular Bavarian saint, whose life is said to have spanned 150 years, we find a core tradition of a missionary monk who worked to improve the physical as well as spiritual conditions of the people in his care. A stranger named Tozzo convinced Magnus and another monk to leave the safety of the monastery of St Gall to evangelize the Allgäu region of Bavaria. One by one, the companions dropped away, leaving Magnus to push forward to Füssen alone. He not only brought his adopted people the Word of eternal life but words for this life as well. His instruction lifted up their souls in faith, and also helped lift their lives out of the poverty they were suffering from by teaching them how to improve crop production and mine a local mountain.

OTHER SAINTS · DONATIAN AND OTHERS · LIBERATUS OF LORO

Lawrence (kneeling) pictured with a group of other saints.

7

SOZON
Martyr d.304?

Tradition says that a shepherd of Cilicia, who had taken the name Sozon in baptism, broke the hand of a golden idol with only his shepherd's crook and divided the gold among the poor. When he heard that innocent people had been arrested for his sacrilege, he hurried to court to confess. The governor told him that he would be set free if he worshipped the now one-handed idol. Sozon declared that he refused to worship a god who couldn't protect himself against a shepherd's crook. Before he was executed he was forced to walk with nails driven into his sandals but his faith enabled him to keep his humour and good spirits. He pointed out that the crimson blood on his legs made much brighter boots than even the governor wore.

OTHER SAINTS · REGINA · JOHN OF NICODEMIA · CLOUD

8

ADRIAN AND NATALIA
Martyrs d.304?

Natalia, according to legend, was the young Christian bride of a Roman officer named Adrian who, though not a Christian, admired his wife's spiritual, as well as physical, beauty. Adrian was so moved by the courage of the persecuted Christians he guarded that he demanded to be counted as one of the warriors of Christ and was arrested. Natalia, concerned more for her husband's soul than his body, hurried to prison to beg the other Christians to instruct him in the faith. She nursed her husband and the other prisoners after their torture, even dressing as a man when women were forbidden to enter the prison. She held her husband's hand when he was executed. When a tribune sought to marry the young widow, she fled to Byzantium, where she died after an arduous journey.

OTHER SAINTS · KIERAN OF CLOMACNOIS · SERGIUS I · CORBINIAN

9

PETER CLAVER
Jesuit priest and patron of Missions to African Americans b.1581?, d.1654

When this Jesuit missionary arrived in Colombia, he entered the same port of Cartagena that each year welcomed slave ships carrying 10,000 kidnapped West Africans who were chained, starved, beaten, and neglected so horribly that over one-third of them died on each voyage. Peter's background as the shy son of a Spanish farmer seemed to be an inadequate indication for a missionary life, but the Jesuit doorkeeper, St Alphonsus Rodriguez, inspired him to push his request to go to the New World on his reluctant superiors. After being ordained in Cartagena, he joined the group of priests led by Father Alfonso de Sandoval who valiantly endured the harassment of traders and local authorities to minister to the Africans. Peter proclaimed himself the

"Peter...visited the plantations to promote better treatment of the blacks, staying with the Africans in their slave quarters."

"slave of the Africans" and said that he must speak to the Africans with his hands before he could speak with his mouth. So, whenever a slave ship entered the harbour, Peter was waiting on the docks with his assistants, eager to bring food, medicine, and comfort to the frightened, tortured people in the stinking holds or crowded pens. He enlisted several interpreters, and used his own knowledge of Angolan as well as pictures to communicate Jesus' teachings. Every year he visited the plantations to promote better treatment of the blacks, staying with the Africans in their slave quarters, in spite of the disgruntled planters who looked on prayer as a disruption of labour. Peter told the wealthy patrons attracted by his holiness that they would not only have to swallow their prejudice and enter the same confessional used by his black patrons but they would also have to wait until he had absolved all the slaves first. Broken by illness, Peter was confined to bed during the last four years of his life, forgotten and ignored, until word of his approaching death brought crowds seeking blessing and relics.

OTHER SAINTS · GORGONIUS · AUDOMARUS · WULFHILDA

SERVVS · TVVS
SVM · E GO
ET · FILI VS · A

⟶ 10 ⟵

NICHOLAS OF TOLENTINO
Augustinian friar and healer b.1245, d.1305

The safest place in Tolentino, which was an Italian city being torn apart by civil violence between the rival pro-pope Guelphs and pro-emperor Ghibellines, was behind the monastery walls where Nicholas lived as an Augustinian friar. But, although this was the case, during his whole life Nicholas never intentionally made the safe or comfortable choice. Born to a couple who had long been childless, he entered an Augustinian monastery at the age of 11. He struggled with, and eventually rejected, the offer of a more comfortable life by an uncle in a more relaxed order. When he was assigned the duty of distributing alms to the poor who came begging at the monastery, he gave so generously that he even handed out food that was meant for the

"Nicholas...spoke to people in words they could understand instead of showing off his considerable education and erudition."

friars themselves. In Tolentino, the young priest was appointed to preach in the streets, an assignment he eagerly fulfilled every day despite the threats of violence. He spoke directly to the people in words they could understand instead of showing off his considerable education and erudition. Though many were converted by his words, he was often heckled by sceptics in the crowd, including one man who even fenced to distract the listeners. But, day after day, this heckler couldn't fail to notice how patiently Nicholas dealt with the disturbance, and he couldn't help but hear some of what Nicholas said. One day the words found a home in his heart and he reformed his life. Nicholas also entered the ghettoes to nurse the sick and reconcile feuding neighbours and family, where he gained a reputation as a healer. When he suffered his final illness, he learned that a man he had long sought to convert would only confess to him. Though the safety of his health dictated that he stay in bed, his duty helped him summon the strength to minister to one more person in need before he died.

OTHER SAINTS • FINNIAN OF MOVILLE • SALVIUS OF ALBI

St Nicholas connected easily with ordinary people.

⟶ 11 ⟵

THEODORA OF ALEXANDRIA
Desert mother and hermit Fifth century

Emulating St Anthony and other desert hermits, Theodora withdrew to the Egyptian desert and became renowned for her wisdom, which is preserved in maxims and parables. To those who thought the Gospel negated the need to follow God's law, she responded that by following His law we show we belong to the One who created both us and the law. She described a hermit who sought to escape his temptations by going elsewhere only to find that a double, his Self, travelled with him wherever he went. She also told of devils who explained that they weren't driven away by fasting because they didn't eat, nor all-night vigils because they didn't sleep, nor solitude because isolation brought opened the way to despair. Only humility made them flee.

OTHER SAINTS • PAPHNUTIUS • PATIENS OF LYONS • DEINIOL

⟶ 12 ⟵

GUY OF ANDERLECHT
Pilgrim d.1012

Guy worked as a field labourer, praying for the grace to love his impoverished circumstances, until he felt called to an even more austere life as a hermit. Wandering to Laekan, he became a sacristan who quietly and faithfully fulfilled his responsibilities to care for the church. He was lured away from this simple life by a get-rich-quick trading scheme that he hoped would provide money for the poor. When this ended in disaster, he realized his error in trusting in the world, and took a pilgrimage to the Holy Land in reparation. On the way, he met up with the dean of Anderlecht and decided to faithfully accompany him, which he did until the dean died. After seven years, Guy returned to Brussels, so worn out from the hardships of his journey that he died in the house of a poor peasant.

OTHER SAINTS • AILBE • SIX MARTYRS OF OMURA

13

JOHN CHRYSOSTOM
Bishop and Doctor of the Church b. 350?, d. 407

John's preaching and writing may have won him the title of "chrysostom", or "golden-tongued," after his death, but the honesty of his words inspired hatred as well as love during his lifetime. He became a priest in his hometown of Antioch after an experience as a hermit convinced him that he was called to service the community. Antioch was so attached to the gifted preacher who had averted reprisals after a riot that the emperor had to move John to his position as bishop of Constantinople secretly. As bishop, John built hospitals and organized deaconesses to help the poor. But his zeal to reform the clergy and the imperial court resulted in his exile. He continued to write and speak out from banishment until he died from the hardships of his punishment.

OTHER SAINTS • MARCELLINUS OF CARTHAGE • AMATUS

14

NOTBURGA OF TYROL
Cook and feeder of the poor b. 1265, d. 1313

From the age of 18, Notburga served as cook for the Count of Rottenburg in his castle in Tyrol. At the end of every day she gave the leftovers from their meals to the poor. When the count's son, Henry, succeeded his father, his thrifty wife, Odilia, ordered Notburga to give the scraps to the pigs instead of the poor. Notburga deprived herself of food to provide for the needy but was fired when Odilia suspected Notburga of disobeying her orders about the scraps. Notburga worked for a farmer at the foot of the Alps until Henry, about to remarry after Odilia's death, called her back to the castle, regretting the loss of her cooking as much as her unfair dismissal. She continued to serve her employer faithfully as well as reaching out and helping the poor generously until she died.

OTHER SAINTS • ALBERT OF JERUSALEM • PETER OF TARENTAISE

John Chrysostom became bishop of Constantinople.

15

CATHERINE OF GENOA

Mystic and nurse b.1447, d.1510

As the daughter of one of the most powerful families in Italy, Catherine was destined to be the subject of an arranged marriage. But the match that considered every political and financial benefit completely ignored the incompatibility of the parties involved. Catherine was beautiful and intelligent but too intense and serious for her passionate, spendthrift husband, Giuliano Adorno, who preferred to spend time with his mistress. Ten years of loneliness led Catherine to chronic depression. During her Lenten confession in 1473, desolation made her speechless and she ran home. Suddenly she was overwhelmed with an experience of the love of God that not only lifted her out of despair but shifted her focus from herself to God and her neighbour.

"she...produced writings on purgatory and a dialogue between the soul and the body, [and] was also a practical administrator."

Strengthened by prayer, she devoted herself to serving the sick in the slums and hospitals, dressing wounds, changing sick beds, and comforting the suffering. Meanwhile her husband's spending led to his bankruptcy. This disgrace and his wife's patience brought about the reform of his life and he joined his wife in serving the poor. Eventually the couple moved into the hospital where they worked. Though she was a mystic who produced writings on purgatory and a dialogue between the soul and body, Catherine was also a practical administrator. As director of the hospital for several years, she kept accounts so well that they were never wrong by even a penny. After Giuliano's death in 1497, Catherine used his remaining money to help the poor as well as provide for Giuliano's former mistress and their illegitimate daughter. In her writings, which influenced St Francis de Sales and St John of the Cross, she described the search throughout the world for something that would satisfy both soul and self-love. She described how the constant battle between the spirit and the body was resolved in the Eucharist, where both could feel alive.

OTHER SAINTS • NICOMEDES • VALERIAN • AICHARDUS

16

CORNELIUS AND CYPRIAN OF CARTHAGE

Pope and bishop, martyrs d.253/b.200?, d.258

Cyprian was a dynamic lawyer in Carthage who converted at the age of 45 and became a priest. As bishop of Carthage during the Decian persecution, he was forced to govern his diocese from hiding. Many Christians apostatized under threat of death then later wished to return to the church. Cornelius, the pope, recommended compassion that would allow them back after penance. Cyprian's support helped him derail opposition that believed former apostates should be kept out. Under renewed persecution, Cornelius was exiled and died of the hardships of imprisonment. When Cyprian refused to participate in pagan worship under Valerian's edict, he was banished then executed.

OTHER SAINTS • EUPHEMIA • NINIAN • LUDMILA • EDITH OF WILTON

17

ROBERT BELLARMINE

Cardinal and Doctor of the Church b.1542, d.1621

Though this Jesuit priest chose to specialize in theological controversies during a period filled with bitter disputes, he was often the voice of moderation, believing that the middle way held more truth than extremes. His lectures at Louvin developed into a three volume work on theological disputes so thorough that people didn't believe it had been written by one man. He contributed to a revision of the Vulgate version of the Bible and the Catechism of Christian Doctrine before being appointed theologian to the pope. Though the position may sound dry, it was very risky, requiring great diplomacy and discernment in dealing with delicate decisions that could split the church. No ivory-tower theologian, he also spent several years as bishop of Capua working for adult instruction, clergy reform, and social justice.

OTHER SAINTS • LAMBERT OF MAASTRICHT • HILDEGARD OF BINGEN

18

JOSEPH OF CUPERTINO

Franciscan friar and patron of aviation and astronauts b.1603, d.1663

Born into poverty, Joseph was beaten by his mother and derided by other children for his stupidity. His clumsiness resulted in his dismissal from an apprenticeship and a Capuchin monastery. He became a stable hand in a Franciscan convent where his humility so impressed the friars that he was admitted and ordained a priest. But his superiors soon restricted his contact with the public and his community because of his eccentricity. The mention of God or the notes of hymns sent him into ecstasies and there were reports of levitation, including leaps in the air to hug the tabernacle during Mass. These phenomena attracted unwelcome attention from the Inquisition. He was shuffled from friary to friary, but responded to harsh treatment with humility.

OTHER SAINTS • FERREOLUS • RICHARDIS • LAMBERT OF FREISING

19

JANUARIUS

Bishop and martyr d.305?

There is early evidence that Januarius was a bishop martyred near Naples. Legends say he was bishop of Benevento when his close friend, the deacon Sossos, was arrested with other Christians during the persecution of Diocletian. Januarius visited his friend in prison and was arrested, along with his deacon and lector who rushed to support him. All the Christians were driven before the governor in chains and exposed to beasts in the amphitheatre. When the animals wouldn't touch them, the martyrs were beheaded. Januarius is associated with a miracle that supposedly still occurs at the chapel in Naples, which preserves a vial of his blood and his head. The congealed blood in the vial melts, bubbles, and begins to flow when brought close to the shrine containing the head on special feast days.

OTHER SAINTS • PELEUS AND COMPANIONS • MARY OF CERVELLÓN

20

ANDREW KIM TAE-GON, PAUL CHONG HA-SANG, AND COMPANIONS

Martyrs of Korea d.1839 to 1867

The first Catholic community in Korea was formed by Yi Sung-hun, a Korean scholar impressed by what he'd read of Christianity. One Korean Christian, Paul Chong Ha-sang, travelled to Beijing to appeal for missionaries and smuggled Bishop Laurent Imbert and two priests into Korea under growing persecution. Fresh violence broke out, so the bishop and priests surrendered in the unsuccessful hope of saving lay Christians but they were all martyred. In 1845, Andrew, who had been sent to a Chinese seminary, returned as the first native Korean priest, but was beheaded within a year. The executions continued until 1886 and 103 martyrs are honoured on this day.

OTHER SAINTS • METHODIUS OF OLYMPUS • JOHN CHARLES CORNAY

21

MATTHEW

Apostle and evangelist First century

Matthew, named by the Synoptic Gospels as one of the 12 Apostles, was a tax collector in Capernaum when Jesus commanded him to follow him. Calling Matthew was a bold step for Jesus because tax collectors were hated for charging more than the prescribed tax. Matthew immediately left his work and threw a banquet for Jesus, inviting other tax collectors. When the Pharisees and scribes criticized Jesus for eating with sinners, Jesus responded that he had come to call the sinners not the righteous. Various traditions relate that after Pentecost Matthew preached in Judea, Ethiopia, Persia, or Macedonia. The earliest authorities seem to agree that he died a natural death. The Gospel that bears his name was compiled in the last half of the first century and transcribed in Greek in about 80AD.

OTHER SAINTS • MICHAEL OF CHERNIGOV AND THEODORE

Matthew (right) immediately followed Jesus, leaving his lucrative tax collecting career behind and inviting other collectors to join with them.

22

THOMAS OF VILLANOVA
Archbishop b.1488, d.1555

Thomas learned his lifelong generosity from his parents who made bread for the poor and encouraged his childhood attempts to save his own food for the needy. Thomas was such an impressive student that the University of Alcala appointed him professor of philosophy at the early age of 26. His heart called him to a different life, however, and he joined the Augustinians in 1518. After ordination, his leadership abilities led to his appointments as prior and provincial, and finally to his election as archbishop of Valencia, which he accepted only under order by his superiors. He walked on foot to his new diocese wearing an old habit. During his installation, he tossed aside the cushions and rugs to kneel on the bare floor and embrace the cross. His first

"He ...took his vow of poverty seriously, refusing to replace his oft-mended habit. Two-thirds of his income went to the poor."

act as bishop was to visit the local prisons and mandate improvements in their conditions. When his cathedral staff gave him money to purchase new furnishings, he immediately sent the money to a hospital, saying that the donation would serve God better there. To their disgust he still took his vow of poverty seriously, refusing to replace his oft-mended habit. Two-thirds of his income went to the poor. To those who complained that some of the hundreds who received food at his door each day might be undeserving of his help, he replied that it was the responsibility of the police to ferret out people's dishonesty but his duty was to help anyone who came to him in need. He had a particular compassion for foundlings, rewarding his servants for each baby they saved and keeping track of the care each infant received. He exhorted the rich to follow his example, saying that it was better to be rich in mercy than in earthly possessions. As he lay dying, he gave away all his money and possessions, including the very bed he lay on, although he asked if he could borrow it until he died.

OTHER SAINTS • PHOCAS OF SINOPE • MAURICE AND COMPANIONS

23

ADAMNAN OF IONA
Abbot b.623?, d.704

This abbot of Iona negotiated the freedom of 60 Irish captives in Northumbria. Afterwards, he framed "Adamnan's Law" to prohibit the capture or killing of non-combatants in battle. He was close friends with Aldfrith, before the man was crowned King of Northumbria, and Aldfrith was known as "foster-son of Adamnan." This learned scholar wrote a life of St Columba, important for its historical perspective, and an early description of the Holy Land, based on the adventures of a Frankish bishop shipwrecked in the British Isles. Though Adamnan wholeheartedly accepted the Roman calculation of Easter and spread this practice to other monasteries in his travels, his own monks at Iona refused to adopt the change.

OTHER SAINTS • LINUS

24

GERARD OF SAGREDO
Bishop and martyr d.1046

Gerard had been planning to pass through Hungary on his pilgrimage to the Holy Land, but he never got to Jerusalem. St Stephen, King of Hungary, impressed by the scholarship of this Benedictine monk from Venice, persuaded Gerard to stay to tutor his son. But Gerard soon showed that his preaching abilities were more invaluable in converting the Hungarians to Christianity and he was appointed first bishop of Csanad. When Stephen died, struggles for power erupted, and inflamed persecution of Christians. Gerard's party was ambushed by supporters of one of the anti-Christian leaders while returning from a celebration of Mass. As Gerard prayed in the words of the first St Stephen that this sin should not be held against his attackers, he was pierced by a lance and his body thrown into the Danube.

OTHER SAINTS • GEREMARUS • PACIFICO OF SAN SEVERINO

⟫•25•⟪

CEOLFRITH OF WEARMOUTH
Abbot and scholar b.647?, d.716

In days of limited communication, Ceolfrith learned by travelling, studying ecclesiastical and monastic knowledge while on journeys to monasteries throughout England. Impressed by his scholarship, St Benedict Biscop invited the monk to Wearmouth and later appointed him abbot of its sister house, Jarrow. Ceolfrith's dedication to liturgy was so strong that after a plague killed everyone at Jarrow except Ceolfrith and a student, who was later known as St Bede, the two sang the Divine Office by themselves. After succeeding Benedict, he transformed Wearmouth into a celebrated centre of learning. He died in France aged 74, after failing to make one last trip to Rome.

OTHER SAINTS • AUNACHARIUS • SERGIUS OF RADONEZH

⟫•26•⟪

COSMAS AND DAMIAN
Martyrs and patrons of surgeons and barbers d.287?

Though no facts are known for certain about these martyrs, they probably died for their faith at Cyrrhus in Syria where a basilica was erected in their honour. The earliest story describes them as brothers from Arabia who were doctors. Later legends say that they accepted no money for their services. Arrested with three other brothers, Anthimius, Leontius, and Euprepius, for their faith, they were interrogated by the governor of Cilicia who promised to release them if they would worship idols. When the brothers rejected this offer they were tortured and then beheaded. On the rack, Cosmas argued that the gods couldn't be enraged at Christians because how could stone be angry?

OTHER SAINTS • COLMÁN ELO • TERESA COUDERC

Sts Cosmas and Damian heal Deacon Justinianus.

27

VINCENT DE PAUL

Founder of Ladies of Charity and Vincentians b.1581, d.1660

Vincent was always looking for a good opportunity. At first, the priesthood was simply a lucrative career to lift him out of poverty but gradually his attention turned to finding ways to serve God. One day, he mentioned a sick family in a sermon to his parish. He arrived at the family's house after Mass to find that parish women had arrived before him and left provisions. Vincent saw the opportunity to form the Ladies of Charity to help those in need. After a wealthy family requested his help to instruct the peasants on their estates, he organized a congregation of priests to help, which became the Priests of the Mission or Vincentians. In the years that followed, he established hospitals, seminaries, orphanages, and soup kitchens.

OTHER SAINTS • SIGEBERT

28

WENCESLAUS

Martyr and patron of Czechoslovakia b.907?, d.929?

The Duke of Bohemia, Wenceslaus, was educated by his grandmother, St Ludmila, who, with her husband, introduced Christianity to Bohemia. After facing challenges from his own mother, Wenceslaus used his authority to spread Christianity, establishing churches in every city and inviting priests to Bohemia. He demonstrated charity not only in works of mercy, but also in reforms such as banning torture for interrogation and dismantling gallows. His Christianity and an alliance with Germany alienated pagan nobles who turned to his brother Boleslas. Boleslas invited his brother to his home where he attacked him. As Wenceslaus fell under the blows of his brother's servants, he prayed for God's forgiveness on his brother. The 19th-century carol "Good King Wenceslas" has no relation to any recorded event of Wenceslaus's life.

OTHER SAINTS • LAWRENCE RUIZ AND COMPANIONS

29

CHARLES DE BLOIS

Soldier and biographer of the saints b.1319, d.1364

Though he longed for religious life in his youth, the circumstances of his aristocratic birth and his marriage to the niece of the King of Brittany led Charles to the battlefield, not the monastery. When rival claims to Brittany escalated into war, Charles never forgot the human beings affected by battle. After conflicts, he supplied food for the inhabitants, cared for the wounded, and arranged prayers for the dead. He deferred conflict on Sunday, explaining that they could always acquire cities but could not recover from missing Mass. Captured in 1354, Charles was imprisoned in the Tower of London by his rival's allies. His nine years of captivity were spent in prayer and writing a biography of St Ivo. He returned to France only to die in battle the next year.

30

JEROME

Priest and Doctor of the Church b.345?, d.420

Jerome was a man of extremes. He inspired lifelong devotion in friends like St Paula and St Eusebius, who both left their homes to establish monastic communities with him in Bethlehem. But he also made bitter enemies with his vehement written attacks against those with whom he disagreed. An educated scholar who loved languages, he nevertheless gave up his beloved classics to focus his life's work on the Scriptures when a vision of Christ accused him of being more of a Ciceronian than a Christian. He produced volumes of biblical commentaries and a new Latin version of the Bible based on the original texts, known as the Vulgate. Yet he always dropped this work to care for refugees fleeing the sack of Rome, saying that it was more important to translate the Scripture into action than into Latin.

OTHER SAINTS • GREGORY THE ENLIGHTENER • SIMON OF CRÉPY

The meditation of St Jerome.

1

THERESE OF LISIEUX
(TERESA OF THE CHILD JESUS)

Carmelite nun and patroness of Missions b.1873, d.1897

Many Catholics have found more inspiration in the "Little Flower" than in a thousand theologians. At 15, Therese was so determined to join her sisters in the Carmelite convent that she spoke up during a papal audience to ask the pope for his support. She realized great deeds were beyond her life but believed she could be a saint despite her "littleness." So she scattered spiritual flowers of sacrifices filled with love – smiling at people she didn't like, taking blame for things she didn't do, accepting leftovers without complaint. But her greatest sacrifice was when she fell ill with tuberculosis. As she lay dying she promised she would spend her heaven on earth, helping those she left behind.

OTHER SAINTS • ROMANUS THE MELODIST • MYLOR • BAVO

2

ANTONY CHEVRIER

Priest and founder b.1826, d.1879

Antony was working as a pastor in Lyons when the Rhone River overflowed, leaving many people homeless. He immediately pitched in to help alleviate the tragedy and continued to serve after the immediate danger was past by ministering at a refuge for those who lost everything in the floods. This experience revealed to him crises that the poor were confronted by every day, not just in times of disaster. He established the Providence of the Prado in an old ballroom to shelter abandoned children and other needy people and founded communities of priests and sisters to minister to his guests. Through his writings, he encouraged other priests to live a life guided by prayer and dedicated to serving the poor, to focus on the unique vocation of priests while leaving other responsibilities of their parish or apostolate to lay people.

OTHER SAINTS • ELEUTHERIUS OF NICOMEDIA • LEGER

St Francis before the pope, who was approving his writing.

3

THOMAS OF HEREFORD

Bishop b.1218, d.1282

Thomas was always ready to jump into the middle of a fight, either as peacemaker or as defender of rights, including his own. As chancellor of Oxford, he waded into violent student conflicts to confiscate weapons. He was exiled for supporting the rights of the barons against Henry III. After making peace with Henry he returned as chancellor of England and was consecrated bishop of Hereford in 1275. He was so zealous in his pastoral duties that he would jump off his horse to confirm children he saw on the road. His defence of his rights as bishop resulted in a bitter quarrel with the archbishop of Canterbury. Thomas died in Rome, where he had gone to get the pope's support.

OTHER SAINTS • HEWALD THE WHITE AND HEWALD THE BLACK

4

FRANCIS OF ASSISI

Founder of the Order of Friars Minor (Franciscans) b.1182, d.1226

When Francis heard Jesus telling him to "repair his church," he changed from being the charming "life-of-the-party," becoming instead a beggar preaching in the streets. He believed he was called to imitate Jesus through a life of holy poverty, possessing nothing but God's love. He followed the Gospel so literally that he made one of his followers offer his robe to the thief who had stolen his hood! Poverty brought freedom and consequently joy to Francis and his followers. But as the Order grew, many tried to change his dream. Francis gave up responsibility for his Order and became the simple brother he had always wanted to be. After he lost his eyesight, he wrote his great *Canticle of the Sun* expressing his brotherhood with creation, including Brother Death who he knew was soon to welcome him.

OTHER SAINTS • AMMON OF NITRIA • PETRONIUS OF BOLOGNA

RAYMOND OF CAPUA
Dominican priest b.1330, d.1399

At first, Raymond was not certain what to make of the young woman who said God had sent Raymond to help her. But as cautious as he was to accept St Catherine of Siena's visions, he also never criticized things he didn't understand. Raymond, a 44-year-old Dominican friar, was indeed the person Catherine needed to give her stability and direction. Though his name has become inextricably linked to hers because of his support of her mission and the biography he wrote, he had his own vocation. As master general of the Dominicans he repaired the devastation caused to the Order during the plague by emphasizing monastic discipline and spirituality. He also encouraged the Dominican Third Order for lay people.

OTHER SAINTS • APOLLINARIS OF VALENCE • FLORA OF BEAULIEU

6

BRUNO
Founder of the Carthusians b.1035?, d.1101

For 20 years, Bruno had built up a successful academic and ecclesiastical career that included directing the celebrated cathedral school of Rheims. But Bruno could not stomach serving as chancellor to the bishop of Rheims, who espoused the belief that his lucrative position would be perfect if only he didn't have to celebrate Mass. When Bruno and others failed to remove the bishop, Bruno became convinced that he would never find inner peace unless he removed himself from the grasping nature of worldly success. With six companions, he appealed to a former student, the Bishop St Hugh of Grenoble, for a place to establish their monastery. Hugh granted them his own alpine retreat at Chartreuse, which then became the first monastery of the Carthusian Order. The austere life amid breathtaking beauty served, as

Bruno described it, to clear and purify their vision in order for them to be able to discern God. In their cells each one of them prayed, read, and worked on transcribing manuscripts. The purpose of the manual work was to allow the monks to reach an inner stillness through their quiet activity. But Pope Urban II, another former student, then destroyed Bruno's quiet happiness by calling him to travel to Rome as a councillor. Bruno's six companions begged him to allow them to accompany him to Rome, but they soon became depressed by the dirt and noise of the city that they found there and fled back to their mountain life. The pope, unfortunately, by this time had come to depend on Bruno and refused to give him permission to leave also. In 1094, Bruno was able to escape to La Torre, which, though not his beloved Alps, still provided a quiet retreat for him. He died peacefully while still at the community he had established there.

OTHER SAINTS • NICETAS OF CONSTANTINOPLE

7

ARTALDUS
Bishop b.1101?, d.1206

When Artaldus was 20 years old, he felt the call of the solitary life over the pomp of the court of Duke Amadeus III, where he had been for two years. He became a Carthusian monk at Portes, which was where he was ordained a priest. Ten years later he was sent to found a new charterhouse (as Carthusian abbeys were called) in Val Romey near the castle where he had been born. When their first buildings were destroyed by fire, Artaldus and his six companions started to build again on the Arvières river. Many people, including the pope, asked for Artaldus's advice and, when he was 80, the pope forced him to leave his beloved solitude to serve as bishop of Belley. He was allowed to resign two years later and returned to the monastery to live the rest of his days in peace.

OTHER SAINTS • JUSTINA • HELAN OF CORNWALL • OSYTH

8

KEYNE

Missionary and founder Sixth century?

This Welsh saint refused every marriage offer to consecrate her life to God. Travelling through Cornwall and south Wales, and possibly Herefordshire and Somerset, she left chapels and legends that mark her spiritual and physical journey. In Keynsham, tradition says that the fossil ammonites are snakes that her prayer turned to stone. Her nephew, St Cadoc, eventually went looking for her and took her home to Llageneu in Abergavenny where she built a hermitage at the foot of the mountain. Her prayer brought forth a spring there famous for its healing powers. Robert Southey's ballad records another legend – that whichever member of a couple drinks from a well dedicated to her in Cornwall will be the ruler of the marriage.

OTHER SAINTS • PELAGIA • DEMETRIUS

9

DENIS AND COMPANIONS

Martyrs d.286?

In the sixth century St Gregory of Tours provided the earliest information on these popular French saints. About the year 250, seven Italian bishops, including Denis (also known as Dionysius or Denys), were sent by the pope as missionaries to Gaul. Denis preached the Gospel with a priest named Rusticus and a deacon named Eleutherius. Their success drew the hostility of the pagan authorities who imprisoned and beheaded them. The chapel that was built over their graves was replaced by the abbey of Saint-Denis in the seventh century. Denis, who is considered the first bishop of Paris and the patron of France, has been confused with Dionysius the Areopagite. According to legend, Denis lived in the Parisian home of one of his first converts, a noble named Lisbius, the ancestor of the Montmorency family.

OTHER SAINTS • JOHN LEONARDI • DIONYSIUS THE AREOPAGITE

St Denis preaching in Gaul.

10

FRANCIS BORGIA

Jesuit priest, husband, and father b.1510, d.1572

Two disastrous military campaigns and a close experience with the aftermath of death convinced Francis Borgia, whose family had a notorious history, to take a spiritual path even if his responsibilities kept him in the world. As governor of Catalonia he routed brigands, reformed a corrupt judicial system, and established schools and hospitals. After his wife died and his children were settled, he joined the Jesuits. He rarely enjoyed the seclusion he desired because his talents were too valuable to the church. As general of the Jesuits, Francis put the young society on a firm foundation by expanding to Poland, France, and the Spanish colonies. While leading a public life, he developed a contemplative life so rich that Teresa of Avila sought his advice on prayer.

OTHER SAINTS • CERBONIUS OF PIOMBINO • AULINUS OF YORK

11

BRUNO THE GREAT

Archbishop of Cologne b.925, d.965

Bruno, the son of Henry the Fowler, the King of Germany, and St Matilda, worked closely with his brother King Otto I to strengthen Germany spiritually and politically. The positions of trust Bruno received would qualify as nepotism except that he was always the best choice for the job. When given two abbeys at the age of 15, he reformed the discipline of both. As archbishop of Cologne, he didn't neglect his pastoral duties for the demands of imperial politics. He promoted learning and discipline among the clergy, visited churches frequently, and provided an example with his own life. When his brother gave him the duchy of Lorraine, Bruno acted as a peacemaker among warring parties. So trusted a leader was he that Otto appointed him co-regent when he went to Rome to be crowned emperor.

OTHER SAINTS • NECTARIUS OF CONSTANTINOPLE • MARY SOLEDAD

Edward the Confessor was known for his holiness.

12

WILFRID OF YORK

Bishop b.634, d.709

Wilfrid arrived at the Northumbrian court with a full retinue, but left with an old noble who convinced him to enter the monastery of Lindisfarne. As Wilfrid studied, he hungered to go to the source of scholarship and made his first journey to Rome. His election as bishop of York became confused when St Chad was also appointed. Wilfrid retired humbly to Ripon monastery until the issue was decided in his favour. His support of the centralized church over the national church put him in conflict with kings and archbishops resulting in several exiles and appeals to Rome. But his troubles never interfered with pastoral opportunities. On one journey he spread the Gospel to the Frisians and, while exiled in Sussex, helped end a famine by teaching locals how to fish.

OTHER SAINTS • MAXIMILIAN OF LORCH • FELIX AND CYPRIAN

13

EDWARD THE CONFESSOR

King of England b.1005?, d.1066

After Edward was elected King of England in 1042, he brought stability and peace to a country that had been torn apart by the power struggles between English and Danish political forces. He avoided armed conflict whenever possible, forming an alliance with his chief rival, Earl Godwin, through marriage. When Godwin later rebelled, Edward not only settled the conflict peacefully but used the counsel of his former enemy and his son to strengthen his country. Though he angered some by his dependence on Norman support, his reputation for holiness grew from his devotion to spiritual matters, generosity to the poor and strangers, and cures affected by his touch. To the great joy of the people, he lifted a burdensome tax after, according to legend, he saw a demon dancing on the heap of gold collected.

OTHER SAINTS • GERALD OF AURILLAC • DANIEL AND COMPANIONS

MISERICORDIAS DOMINI · IN ETERNVM CANTABO

B.V. ERESA. DE JESVS;

8 ANNO SVÆ
ÆTATIS
· 61 ·
A SALVTIS
1576
DIE ECVDOME
SIS IVNII

14

CALLISTUS I
Pope and martyr d.222

The only contemporary biography of Pope Callistus I was written by a rival, St Hippolytus, who was upset with the mercy Callistus showed to repentant sinners. According to Hippolytus, Callistus was a slave who was accused of embezzling funds and sentenced to forced labour. This is contradicted by the pope's appointment of Callistus to a trusted position. Counselling Pope Zephyrinus on theology led to Callistus's election as pope when Zephyrinus died. The early church had excommunicated sinners guilty of serious sins like murder and adultery but Callistus allowed repentant sinners back if they had performed public penance. By doing this, he said he was following Jesus' example of forgiveness. He is listed as a martyr, but there are no records of this.

OTHER SAINTS • ANGADRISMA

15

TERESA OF AVILA (THERESA OF JESUS)
Founder of the Order of Discalced Carmelites and Doctor of the Church
b.1515, d.1582

Fun-loving Teresa chose religious life because she dreaded the confinement of marriage. In the relaxed Carmelite convent of that era, Teresa was popular with visitors who went there to learn mental prayer but stayed to gossip. She excused herself from praying because she felt she was too sinful until a priest convinced her that that was why she had to pray. Her return to prayer inspired her to reform her life. She set out to restore her Order to its contemplative practice. Her campaign for change led to investigation by the Inquisition, denunciations from the pulpit, and even law suits. But her reform and writings outlasted critics and earned her the title of Doctor of the Church.

OTHER SAINTS • THECLA OF KITZINGEN • RICHARD GWYN

Teresa, having reformed her own life, went on to do the same to her Order.

16

GERARD MAJELLA
Redemptorist brother and patron of pregnant women b.1726, d.1755

Gerard's family had to lock the young tailor in his room because he insisted on following the Redemptorists even though they had rejected him. Escaping with the help of a rope of knotted sheets, he convinced the Redemptorists to take a chance on him. He went on to provide invaluable physical and spiritual support on missions, where crowds sought his advice and reported healing powers. His discernment led to an unusual appointment for a brother as spiritual director for nuns. His prayer life was so profound that he could be heard begging God to release him from contemplation so he could work. After he died of tuberculosis, popular devotion to him as patron of expectant mothers grew worldwide, fuelled by miracles attributed to his intercession.

OTHER SAINTS • GALL • MOMMOLINUS OF NOYON • LULL • HEDWIG

17

IGNATIUS OF ANTIOCH
Bishop and martyr b.37?, d.107

Ignatius, possibly a disciple of St John the Evangelist, was appointed bishop of Antioch about 70AD. When he was 70 years old, Ignatius was denounced as a Christian leader to the emperor and sent to Rome for execution. Manacled and maltreated by soldiers, he was met like royalty by other bishops on his journey to Rome. The letters he wrote to the churches along the way show his concern for unity within the churches. He believed oneness could be achieved through the Eucharist and the authority of the local bishop. He begged the Roman Christians not to request mercy for him because he believed that, just as he had lived his life in imitation of Christ, he must end it the same way, by suffering for the faith. He was put into an amphitheatre and lions devoured him.

OTHER SAINTS • JOHN KOLOBOS • NOTHELM OF CANTERBURY

18

LUKE

Evangelist and patron of physicians First century

Luke, the writer of the Gospel and the Acts of the Apostles, has been identified with St Paul's beloved physician in Colossians 4:14. Luke was possibly a Greek Gentile born in Antioch, and his origins are reflected in his Gospel's focus on evangelizing Gentiles. It also reveals his interest in social justice, his respect for women, and his belief in forgiveness. Luke joined Paul's ministry at Troas in 51AD and travelled with him to Samothrace, Neapolis, and Philippi, where Luke apparently stayed for several years before rejoining Paul in 58AD and travelling with him to Jerusalem. Luke remained with Paul in his final imprisonment (2 Timothy 4:11). The earliest tradition says that Luke died at age 84 in Boeotia after settling in Greece to write his Gospel.

OTHER SAINTS • JUSTUS OF BEAUVAIS

19

JOHN DE BREBEUF AND COMPANIONS

North American martyrs d.1642–49

The six Jesuit priests and their two assistants who are honoured on this day were early French missionaries among the native North Americans. Starting in 1615, small groups of missionaries arrived in Quebec to spread the Gospel. They endured arduous journeys through wilderness to live among the Hurons, sharing their customs and learning their languages. They struggled for years to win the trust of the Native Americans without making a single convert. The missionaries were finally seeing some success with their evangelization when a series of Iroquois attacks against the Hurons resulted in the torture and murder of all but one, Chabanel, who was later killed by a Huron who blamed Christians for his bad fortune.

OTHER SAINTS • PAUL OF THE CROSS • ETHBIN • FRIDESWIDE

St Luke was both a physician and Gospel writer.

MARY BERTILLA BOSCARDIN
Nun b.1888, d.1922

The pain of growing up with a violently abusive father was intensified by neighbours, including her parish priest, who thought the young Bertilla was so stupid that they called her "the goose." Although her schooling had been interrupted so she could help support her poor family by working at home or as a maid, she cherished the seemingly impossible dream of becoming a nun. When she wanted to join the Teachers of St Dorothy, Daughters of the Sacred Heart, the priest thought the most she could contribute to the community was potato peeling. Bertilla, who shared everyone's poor opinion of her abilities, told her novice-mistress that even though she couldn't do anything, she wanted the sister to teach her to be a saint. During her first years

> *"She prayed not for visions or revelations, but simply to work hard for God. Nonetheless, God marked the life of this humble 'goose' with mystical gifts and graces."*

in the religious order, she cheerfully took on the backbreaking, unpleasant tasks in the kitchen and laundry that others shunned. But when she was allowed to nurse children in the hospital at Treviso, the compassion and courage she showed revealed her true talents. During World War I, she ministered with heroic courage to wounded soldiers in the hospital, staying by their beds as heavy artillery barrages exploded all around. Bertilla had not seen the end of misunderstanding, however. One superior underestimated her abilities and sent her back to the laundry, but she was too valuable to be kept there long. After the war she was put in charge of the children's isolation ward in Treviso. She prayed not for visions or revelations, but simply to work hard for God. Nonetheless, God marked the life of this humble "goose" with mystical gifts and graces. She died following surgery for a tumour, and 39 years later patients she had tended with loving compassion saw her canonized.

OTHER SAINTS • CAPRASIUS • ARTEMIUS • ANDREW OF CRETE

HILARION OF GAZA
Hermit b.291?, d.371

Raised as a pagan in Gaza, Hilarion embraced Christianity as a student in Alexandria and went to study with St Antony in the Egyptian desert. He soon became frustrated by the crowds of visitors that made the desert resemble a city and found solitude briefly in Gaza, until fame of his holiness attracted his own crowds of disciples. The monastery, the monks, and the crowds of seekers surrounding him made him feel that he had returned to the world. He left on a fruitless journey to find solitude, travelling to Egypt, Sicily, Dalmatia, and finally Cyprus. Hilarion was the victim of a compassion that wouldn't reject anyone. He never found a wilderness so isolated that it didn't contain a sufferer needing his healing touch who then spread his fame.

OTHER SAINTS • FINTAN OF TAGHMON • JOHN OF BRIDLINGTON

DONATUS OF FIESOLE
Irish writer and teacher d.874?

Donatus was an Irish writer and teacher returning from a pilgrimage to Rome in 829 when he arrived in Fiesole, near Florence. According to tradition, the people in the church were so intent on electing a new bishop that no one noticed the entrance of the short stranger until all the bells started tolling. Whether due to this divine sign or some other reason, the people proclaimed that the stranger should be their new bishop. Donatus served the people who had so immediately adopted him for the rest of his life, but he paid tribute to his first home in poetry extolling the life of St Brigid, Irish scenery, and a hospice dedicated to Brigid. He described himself simply as being a passionate teacher of grammar and writing, but he was also truly a trusted counsellor of popes and rulers.

OTHER SAINTS • ABERCIUS OF HIEROPOLIS • PHILIP OF HERACLEA

23

SEVERINUS BOETHIUS
Philosopher, statesman, and martyr b. 480?, d. 524

Revered as the martyr St Severinus in the Middle Ages, this philosopher and statesman is best remembered as Boethius, the name attached to his influential writings and given to a lunar crater in his honour. His most well-known work, *The Consolation of Philosophy*, was not written by a dreamer in an ivory tower but by a man in prison awaiting execution. Its purpose was not just an intellectual exercise but a practical response to his own struggle. Boethius was the orphan of a Roman patrician family, married the daughter of the senator who raised him, and had two sons who later became consuls. By the age of 30, he had established a distinguished reputation as a scholar. His Latin translations of the classical Greek authors such as Plato and Aristotle, and his own treatises

> *"The Consolation of Philosophy…was not just an intellectual exercise but a practical response to his own struggle."*

and commentaries became the foundation of medieval scholastic theology, logic, and mathematical and musical theory. It was his own study, however, that pushed him out of the library and into public life. He took Plato's statement that the world would be better off if ruled by philosophers as a personal challenge. His practical leadership as consul of Rome led to his appointment by the emperor as master of government and court services in 520. But his worldly success ended abruptly when he was arrested for defending another consul accused of treason. During nine months of imprisonment, Boethius wrote *The Consolation of Philosophy*, a classical dialogue between Boethius and the personified Philosophy, on the classic questions of how evil can seem to prevail if God is good in which he contrasts the human view of "good fortune" with the divine plan of "Providence." Boethius was tortured and executed. Although he was probably not martyred for his faith, as was believed in the Middle Ages, he certainly suffered for upholding Christian principles of justice.

OTHER SAINTS • SEVERINUS OF BORDEAUX • JOHN OF CAPISTRANO

24

ANTONY MARY CLARET
Founder of the Claretians and bishop b. 1807, d. 1870

Antony fits his own description of the ideal Claretian priest who is afire with love and spreads that fire wherever he goes. He organized parish laywomen as evangelists, formed the congregation of Claretian priests, and published millions of books through his religious library. As archbishop of Santiago, Cuba, he persevered against hostile opposition, including an assassination attempt, to establish 53 parishes, found the Claretian Sisters, encourage lay spirituality, and improve the seminary. The worst trial came when he was tied to the Spanish court as the queen's confessor. He used the time to develop his own interior life, preaching missions wherever he travelled. Exiled during a revolution, he was harassed by political opponents until his death in France.

OTHER SAINTS • PROCLUS OF CONSTANTINOPLE • MAGLORIUS

25

CRISPIN AND CRISPINIAN
Martyrs and patrons of shoemakers d. 285?

According to tradition, these two brothers travelled with a band of missionaries from Rome led by St Quintinus to spread the Gospel in Gaul. The brothers settled in Soissons, where they preached by day and worked as shoemakers by night, following St Paul's exhortation that preachers should support themselves instead of depending on alms. When they were denounced as Christians to Maximinus Herculeus, he tried to persuade them to apostatize. When threatened, they said they didn't fear death because their life was Christ. To promises of wealth or position, they said that they had already given up those things for Christ. They were tortured and beheaded, and their bodies thrown into the sewers. Another legend says that they escaped to Faversham in Kent where they lived and worked as shoemakers.

OTHER SAINTS • FORTY MARTYRS OF ENGLAND AND WALES

⟹ 26 ⟸

CEDD
Bishop and missionary d.664

Cedd, the brother of St Chad, was one of four priests from Lindisfarne monastery sent to preach the Gospel in middle England. They accompanied the area's king, Peada, who had converted to Christianity at the request of his father-in-law, the King of Northumbria. Selected for their learning and holy life, the missionaries found willing listeners among nobility and commoners alike. When King Sigebert became Christian, Cedd was called to Essex where he and another priest evangelized the entire countryside. On a visit to Lindisfarne to consult with St Finan, Cedd was consecrated bishop, an authority he used to ordain assistants in evangelization and build churches. He built three monasteries and died at one in Northumbria during a plague.

OTHER SAINTS · RUSTICUS OF NARBONNE · EATA OF HEXHAM

⟹ 27 ⟸

CONTARDO FERRINI
Franciscan tertiary and patron of universities b.1859, d.1902

Having developed a love of learning from his father, who taught mathematics and physics, Contardo became the foremost authority on Roman law and a professor at Borromeo College in Pavia. As devoted as he was to scholarship, he was even more committed to his own spiritual life, becoming a member of the Third Order of St Francis for lay people and living a devoted life of prayer. An avid mountaineer, he saw God revealed in a nature he described as "always smiling in joy to greet its creator." As much as he owed to study, he pointed out that people were much more likely to find God in the colours of a sunset than in knotty intellectual problems. Believing that Catholics should be active out in the world rather than hidden away, he served on the city council of Milan and performed public service.

OTHER SAINTS · AEDESIUS

Severinus Boethius stood up for justice, even when it meant he suffered for doing so.

❧ 28 ❧

SIMON AND JUDE

Apostles First century

Scripture lists Simon and Jude among the 12 Apostles. Simon is described as a Zealot, meaning he was either zealous for Jewish law or a member of the fanatical Zealot party. Jude (also called Judas, Thaddeus, and Lebbeus) asked Jesus at the last supper why he wouldn't reveal himself to the world. The last Scriptural appearance of both is at Pentecost. In Eastern tradition, Simon died peacefully at Edessa while Latin tradition relates that he evangelized Egypt and Persia where he was martyred with Jude. Jude's evolution into the patron of desperate causes is uncertain, but it is suggested that his confusion with Jesus' betrayer (because he has the same name) made him a saint who would only be turned to by someone exhausted of all other hope.

OTHER SAINTS • FIDELIS OF COMO • FARO OF MEAUX

❧ 29 ❧

COLMAN MACDUAGH

Bishop b.550?, d.632?

This son of an Irish chieftain sought solitude as a hermit in Aranmore, where he is credited with building two churches at Kilmurvy. He fled from his election as bishop to hide at Burren in the mountains of County Clare. He became spiritual director for King Guaire of Connaught, who donated the land for the monastery of Kilmacduagh when Colman was finally able to accept the responsibilities of leadership. His rapport with animals is displayed in a tender story of three pets who helped him in his spiritual duties. He not only trained a rooster to announce early morning prayer, but also befriended a mouse who nibbled his ear to wake him for night prayer. His most unusual companion was a bluebottle fly who marked his place in a manuscript if Colman was urgently called away from study.

OTHER SAINTS • NARCISSUS OF JERUSALEM • THEUDERIUS

Jude and Simon with James. Simon is often depicted with a saw as some legends say he was martyred by being sawn in half.

❧ 30 ❧

ALPHONSUS RODRIGUEZ

Jesuit brother b.1533?, d.1617

When his father died, Alphonsus had to leave college to help out in the family wool business in Segovia. A series of personal tragedies, including financial troubles and the deaths of his wife, daughter, and mother, prompted him to turn to a quieter life devoted to God. After his son's death, Alphonsus joined the Jesuits as a lay brother, though he faced initial rejection because of his age (almost 40) and his interrupted education. He held the position of doorkeeper at a Majorca boys' school for 45 years, winning the respect of a variety of visitors who came to his door and sought his advice. Alphonsus was a mystic who devoted himself to union with God whether he was enjoying graces and ecstasies or enduring spiritual desolation and physical suffering.

OTHER SAINTS • SERAPION OF ANTIOCH • GERMANUS OF CAPUA

❧ 31 ❧

WOLFGANG OF REGENSBURG

Bishop b.924?, d.994

Wolfgang helped his friend and fellow Swabian, Henry, from the time they were students, accompanying him on each new appointment, finally serving as chaplain while Henry was bishop of Trier. When Henry died in 964, Wolfgang retired to Switzerland as a Benedictine monk. He was then appointed director of the monastery school and went on to be ordained as priest, go on a mission to Pannonia, and become bishop of Regensburg (Ratisbon) in 972. He reformed two religious communities of women, returned revenues to an abbey that had been impoverished by his predecessors, and ensured that churches were provided with everything they needed to celebrate the Eucharist properly. Famous for his kindness to the poor, he refused to blame a thief dressed in rags who had stolen his bed curtain, making him a present of the cloth.

OTHER SAINTS • QUENTIN • FOILLAN • BEGU

1

RUPERT MAYER
Jesuit Priest b.1876, d.1945

The Nazis had to stop Rupert. The Jesuit priest from Austria was well-loved and respected because of his ministry to workers and students, and the religious associations he had organized in all the parishes in the city. His heroism as a chaplain in World War I cost him his leg but gave him even more credibility. When Rupert refused to be intimidated by harassment and arrests, he was imprisoned in a concentration camp. Later he was interned at a deserted monastery, where he wrote that he truly had no one but God. As soon as he was liberated by American troops, he returned to Munich to minister to his people. In the few months before he died of a stroke, he put all his energy into helping people rebuild their spiritual and physical lives.

OTHER SAINTS • BENIGNUS OF DIJON • CAESARIUS AND JULIAN

2

MARCIAN OF CHALCIS
Hermit d.388?

Marcian wasn't an anti-social loner who went to the desert to escape people but a charming courtier who left Cyprus because he preferred the company of God. In the desert, he devoted himself to a dialogue with God, in which God spoke through Scripture and Marcian answered with prayer. When visiting bishops reprimanded Marcian's stubborn silence during their visit, Marcian responded that with God speaking through creation around them and the Scriptures in front of them, what more could he add? When he broke his fast to eat with a guest, he explained that hospitality took precedence as charity was God's command. Marcian refused to be labelled a miracle-worker, though many were healed despite being turned away by him, and he ordered that his body be buried secretly.

OTHER SAINTS • VICTORINUS

Martin de Porres overcame racial prejudices with his humble sincerity.

3

MARTIN DE PORRES
Dominican brother and patron of social action b.1569, d.1639

The son of a Spanish noble and a free black woman in Peru, Martin overcame prejudice against his mixed race to become a respected healer. When Martin joined the Dominicans at 18 years of age, his loving response to racial insults eventually transformed his enemies into disciples. Formerly employed both as a barber and physician, as was the custom of the time, Martin interpreted his responsibilities as monastery physician broadly, not only nursing his fellow Dominicans back to health, but also taking medicines, food, and spiritual comfort to poor people, and caring for the sick animals who arrived at his door. He gave his own bed to immigrants until they found employment and planted fruit trees along the roads to provide food for travellers.

OTHER SAINTS • WINIFRED • RUMWOLD • HUBERT • PIRMINUS

4

CHARLES BORROMEO
Bishop b.1538, d.1584

At the age of 22, Charles was already papal secretary of state, papal legate, and archbishop of Milan – positions he'd received from his uncle, the pope. Despite a speech impediment, Charles's ecclesiastical career in Rome was assured. But reports about Milan's miserable spiritual condition prompted Charles to do what no bishop of Milan had done for 73 years – actually go to Milan. Charles educated the clergy, established catechism classes, and regulated moral behaviour and the proper use of churches. He also stripped his house and stores to support victims of a plague. He refused to be intimidated, even pushing his way into one church while being fired on by an armed guard. A simple man, he walked out of a feast in his honour because he could only think of the poor that could have been fed with all the food.

OTHER SAINTS • PIERIUS • JOHN ZEDAZNELI AND COMPANIONS

5

ZECHARIAH AND ELIZABETH

Parents of John the Baptist First century

Luke's Gospel paints a portrait of Elizabeth and Zechariah as a married couple both outwardly and inwardly dedicated to God. It was not only Zechariah's position as priest and Elizabeth's heritage as a descendant of the first priest, Aaron, that made them righteous but the way they lived according to all God's commandments. Yet at that time in Palestine, the couple still lived under disgrace because they had no children. The greatest test of their faith was not their childlessness, however, but the way in which their prayers were finally answered. Zechariah was serving his rotation as priest at the temple in Jerusalem when the angel Gabriel appeared to announce that not only would their prayers be fulfilled but that their son was to be named John and would lead many Israelites back to God. Zechariah's scepticism about this promise was punished by his immediate inability to speak. Elizabeth's response was more wholehearted. Six months after she conceived, she recognized her pregnant cousin, Mary, as the mother of Jesus, the Lord. Zechariah redeemed his earlier doubt by insisting, at his son's circumcision, that his son be called John according to the angel's command. Rewarded for his faith with the return of his voice, his first words were in praise of God. Opened now to the Holy Spirit, he prophesied the coming of Jesus and the role of his son in preparing the people for Jesus. Legends say that Elizabeth and Zechariah were in Bethlehem when Herod massacred all the young boys there. Elizabeth escaped with her son to the country where a mountain opened up to hide them. The assassins supposedly murdered Zechariah in the temple when he refused to betray Jesus.

Zechariah and Elizabeth's son, John, was to point the way to Jesus.

OTHER SAINTS • BERTILLA

6

ILLTUD
Abbot Sixth century

This Welsh noble learned that good times could end without warning when his hunting companions were swallowed by a bog, taking his illusions about the permanence of worldly pleasure with them. He established a religious community of men and women, including his wife, but eventually sought greater solitude as a hermit. Later, he organized his disciples into the monastery known as Llaniltud. The depth and breadth of his knowledge was without equal, and he used his learning both to transform his monastery into a celebrated centre of scholarship and introduce an improved method of ploughing to his neighbours. Illtud's nickname, "the Knight," led to legends about his connection to King Arthur and the Holy Grail.

OTHER SAINTS • MELAINE • LEONARD OF NOBLAC • WINNOC

8

GODFREY OF AMIENS
Bishop d.1115

Godfrey's name would never be found among a list of beloved saints. He was so universally disliked he couldn't go anywhere in his diocese without fearing for his life. Godfrey, a Benedictine abbot who was elected bishop of Amiens, alienated the rich by forcing them to exchange their showy clothes for more modest garb in church. He infuriated clergy by enforcing celibacy and rooting out simony. He antagonized religious orders by intervening in abusive practices and punishing an abbess who beat one of her nuns. Only the powerless cared for him as he gave his own dinner to lepers. Frustrated by the enmity directed at him, he tried several times to resign but was always called back. He eventually won his enemies over through his attempts at reform.

OTHER SAINTS • CYBI • DEUSDEDIT • TYSILIO • WILLEHAD

7

ANTONY BALDINNUCCI
Jesuit missionary b.1665, d.1717

Antony joined the Jesuits to be a missionary in the Indies but spent 20 years preaching in his native Italy. Migraines and seizures made his health too precarious for foreign missions. Antony discovered that the Jesuit philosophy of evangelizing using the native culture worked just as well with his own country as in foreign lands. To attract attention in the villages he visited, he carried a cross in elaborate processions. When people followed the parade to the mission, they found Antony using persuasive words instead of sensational spectacles to get his message across. In order to prevent the local thugs from disrupting the mission and to ensure they heard his preaching, he appointed the thugs to keep order. When Antony died after embarking on 448 missions in 20 years, he left behind an Italy renewed in faith by his preaching.

OTHER SAINTS • HERCULANUS • WILLIBRORD • ENGELBERT

9

BENEN OF ARMAGH
Archbishop d.468

According to legend, Benen was a small boy when St Patrick converted his family to Christianity while staying at their house. Benen was so awed by the saint that he scattered flowers over Patrick while he slept. When Patrick left to continue his journey, he found Benen hiding in his chariot, desperate to go with his hero. Benen not only embraced his hero's mission but also developed his own singular talents to further the mission, evangelizing parts of Ireland including Kerry and Clare that Patrick hadn't yet reached. Benen's beautiful voice earned him the title of "Patrick's psalm singer." Benen ruled the monastery of Drumlease, supposedly founded by Patrick, for 20 years. At Patrick's death, he was the unanimous choice of the clergy and laity to replace Patrick as archbishop of Armagh, the Chief See of Ireland.

OTHER SAINTS • VITONUS • RADBOD

10

LEO THE GREAT
Pope and Doctor of the Church d.461

Leo was a deacon on a papal mission to mediate between feuding generals in Gaul when he heard that he had been elected pope himself. As pope, Leo participated actively in the life of the church fulfilling the roles of pastor, peacemaker, teacher, and reformer. The 96 sermons that still survive exhort his flock to charity and social ministry. His letters refute heretical beliefs with clear explanations of Catholic doctrine, especially the Incarnation. When Attila the Hun devastated Italy, Leo convinced him to leave Rome alone in exchange for tribute. He couldn't turn aside the next invader but won Genseric's promise to limit the destruction of life and property. For the five years that remained to Leo, he worked to repair the damage of Genseric's sacking.

OTHER SAINTS • AEDH • JUSTUS • ANDREW AVELLINO

11

MARTIN OF TOURS
Bishop and patron of soldiers b.316?, d.397

After being forced to join the Roman army, Martin ignored insults from his fellow soldiers for cleaning his servant's boots and giving half his cloak to a beggar. But, although Martin was in fact a good soldier, he was imprisoned when he announced that, as a Christian, he couldn't kill anyone. After his release, he lived as a hermit until he was ambushed by crowds in Tours who proclaimed him their new bishop. Martin lived an austere life outside the city in a cabin and travelled from house to house to convert pagans. Martin was so dedicated to freeing prisoners that authorities tried unsuccessfully to avoid him because they knew they couldn't resist his pleas for mercy. When his missions to prevent the execution of heretics in Spain failed, he refused to take communion with the bishops who had ordered the persecution.

OTHER SAINTS • MENNAS • THEODORE THE STUDITE

12

JOSAPHAT OF POLOTSK
Bishop and martyr b.1580?, d.1623

Five centuries after the schism between Eastern and Western churches, six Orthodox bishops in Byelorussia and the Ukraine decided to reunite with Rome. Growing up amid the controversy that erupted over that decision fuelled Josaphat's passion for church unity. After he became the Catholic bishop of Vitebsk and then Polotsk, he introduced synods, a catechism, and rules of clerical conduct. He persevered despite a rival archbishop elected by separatists, conflict with his parishioners, condemnation by the Lithuanian chancellor, and death threats. When a mob attacked his servants, he was killed trying to rescue them. Regret at the murder swung public opinion to unity. Josaphat was the first Eastern-rite bishop canonized by Rome.

OTHER SAINTS • NILUS THE ELDER • EMILIAN CUCULLATUS

13

BRICE OF TOURS
Bishop d.443

Many saints only turned to God after getting a second chance at life. But Brice didn't take his second chance, or his third, or even his fourth. Raised by a saint, Martin of Tours, Brice thought his mentor a fool and a hypocrite. When Brice was accused of improper behaviour for a monk, Martin refused to punish him, saying it would look like revenge. After Martin's death, Brice was elected bishop to replace him, possibly because of his huge wealth and power. Consecration did not reform him and he was forced to leave Tours under clouds of accusations. Seven years of exile in Rome brought about his conversion. When he returned to Tours he was a different bishop – so dedicated to his people, pastoral service, and an austere life that he was proclaimed a saint at his death.

OTHER SAINTS • EUGENIUS OF TOLEDO • MAXELLENDIS • DIDACUS

St Martin travelled to visit those he knew needed God.

— 14 —

LAURENCE O'TOOLE
Archbishop of Dublin b.1128, d.1180

The son of an Irish chieftain, Laurence was taken as a hostage by the cruel King Dermot when he was 10 years old. After Dermot abused him, Laurence was taken to a monastery for safekeeping. He decided to stay and was elected abbot at the age of 25. As archbishop of Dublin he developed a reputation for his firm adherence to monastic life and for generosity, feeding up to 60 poor people a day at his own table. When Dermot, who had been driven from Ireland, returned with English allies, Laurence not only helped the survivors of the Dublin massacre that followed but united the Irish leaders to defend themselves against these invaders. When Henry II produced the papal edict granting Ireland to the English king, Laurence worked to promote peace.

OTHER SAINTS • DYFRIG • NICHOLAS TAVELIC AND COMPANIONS

— 15 —

ALBERT THE GREAT
Bishop and Doctor of the Church b.1206, d.1280

Albert became a Dominican friar even though his powerful family objected. He also advanced scientific study through volumes of writing, lectures at universities in Paris and throughout Germany, and his own research. Called the "universal doctor" by his peers, he was an acknowledged authority on almost every subject including mathematics, science, philosophy, and theology. He mapped European mountain ranges, demonstrated the spherical shape of the earth, and explained why latitude affected climate. Albert laid the foundation for scholastic theology refined by his student, St Thomas Aquinas, by repackaging the banned works of the pagan philosopher Aristotle for Christian minds. Albert humbly faced the worst trial of a great intellect when his memory and mind deteriorated over the last two years of his life.

OTHER SAINTS • DIDIER OF CAHORS • MALO • FINTAN OF RHEINAU

— 16 —

MARGARET OF SCOTLAND
Queen and patroness of Scotland b.1045?, d.1093

This Anglo-Saxon princess took refuge in Scotland after the Norman conquest of England. After marrying her host, King Malcolm III, she used her talents to benefit her adopted country. She was devoted to the education of her eight children, one of whom became a saint, and inspired her husband to follow her example of prayer, virtue, and charity. She also established monasteries, brought the practices of the Scottish Church in harmony with Rome, built hostels for pilgrims, and embroidered liturgical vestments and hangings. By augmenting libraries, corresponding with scholars, and encouraging intellectual discussions, she promoted learning. She died after hearing that her husband and one of her sons had been killed in battle.

OTHER SAINTS • GERTRUDE THE GREAT • MECHTILDIS OF HELFTA

— 17 —

ELIZABETH OF HUNGARY
Wife and mother b.1207, d.1231

Elizabeth was betrothed to Ludwig of Thuringia when they were both babies. Rocked in the same cradle, they grew up loving each other and were married after Ludwig succeeded his father as Landgraf (the equivalent of an earl) at 20. Though willing to dress royally for state occasions, Elizabeth preferred to attend the sick in plain clothes. After Ludwig died in a crusade, her brother-in-law drove her and her three children out of the castle. The only shelter she could find was a shed where she spun thread for a living. Eventually her brother-in-law relented and gave her funds to live on, which she used to build a hospital where she lived and nursed the sick. She suffered under a cruel spiritual director who beat and manipulated her, but he couldn't break her generous heart and she continued to welcome anyone in need.

OTHER SAINTS • DIONYSIUS OF ALEXANDRIA • HILDA OF WHITBY

ROSE PHILIPPINE DUCHESNE

Nun and missionary b. 1769, d. 1852

When Philippine achieved her childhood dream at the age of 49, she didn't realize the hardship its fulfilment would mean for her. As a child, Philippine always longed to be a missionary in America, but obstacles kept pushing the dream farther away from her. She overcame her father's opposition to enter the Visitation convent but was forced to return home when the French Revolution expelled all the nuns. She spent the Revolutionary years ministering to prisoners interned in her former convent. Later, her attempts to start her own congregation in the old convent failed. In 1804 St Madeleine Sophie Barat accepted Philippine and her convent into her new Society of the Sacred Heart but discouraged Philippine's missionary dreams for 14 years

> *"On her last mission to Kansas, the Potawatomie tribe named her 'Woman Who Prays Always.'"*

until Bishop Dubourg of Louisianna requested her help with his frontier diocese. In 1818, Philippine and five other sisters settled in a log cabin near St Louis, Missouri, where they opened the first free school west of the Mississippi. Life was hard but, Philippine said, trials were the riches of the missionaries. The bitter winter froze the milk as it was carried from the barn to the cabin. The community struggled with the language, culture, poverty, and ignorance of the settlers as well as financial difficulties and even slander. But when her brother offered to pay for her return to France, she told him to use the money to find and send two more missionaries to help her instead. 10 years after her arrival she had opened six houses and several schools in Missouri and Louisiana. At 71, Philippine resigned as superior but she never gave up her missionary spirit. On her last mission to Kansas, the Potawatomie tribe named her "Woman Who Prays Always." Unfortunately, she was never able to master their language and she spent her last days in St Louis in prayerful support of her community.

OTHER SAINTS • ROMANUS OF ANTIOCH • MAWES • ODO OF CLUNY

Elizabeth provided for anyone who went to her for help.

19

SALVATOR LILLI AND COMPANIONS

Martyrs d.1895

Salvator was only 20 when the Italian government banned all religious orders. He was forced to go to Palestine to complete his Franciscan novitiate and studies for ordination. In 1880, the young priest was sent to Marasc, Armenia. Though Armenia belonged nominally to Russia it was ruled by Turks who persecuted native Christians. Under this repression, Salvator not only preached tirelessly but also created villages and employment projects. In 1890, the Turkish attacks grew brutal but Salvator would not leave his "sheep" and was arrested along with his parishioners in Mujukderesi. When they refused to renounce Christianity, every one of them was pierced with bayonets.

OTHER SAINTS • NERSES

20

EDMUND

King and martyr b.841, d.869

When the 14-year-old Edmund was proclaimed King of Norfolk, and later of Suffolk (in 855), England had been suffering from Danish raids for decades. Edmund proved to be a wise ruler and devout Christian, memorizing the Psalms of his model King David. When the Danes mounted their largest invasion yet in 866, Edmund first negotiated a peace with them. But after conquering York, the Danes weren't content to leave him alone. Legends say that the Danish leader, Ingvar, proposed joint rule with Edmund but required him to renounce his faith. When Edmund refused, saying he would never buy his life by offending God, the superior forces of the Danes devastated his army and captured him. According to tradition, Edmund was tied to a tree and shot with arrows meant to wound not kill, and was then beheaded.

OTHER SAINTS • DASIUS • BERNWARD

21

MARY SIEDLISKA

Founder of the Congregation of the Holy Family of Nazareth b.1842, d.1902

Though Mary was born in nationalistic Poland and experienced a sheltered upbringing, she felt called to form a religious Order that would cross national borders. Religion was the part of her education that her parents neglected and it took a Capuchin friar, Leander Lendzian, to open her heart to religious life. When a tour of Europe with her family strengthened her desire to serve the universal church, her parents reluctantly gave their blessing. In 1873, Mary received permission to establish the Congregation of the Holy Family of Nazareth. Its members centred their lives on God and each other and their ministry included the care of neglected children, religious instruction, and marriage preparation. Today, 1700 sisters minister in 14 different countries.

OTHER SAINTS • GELASIUS I • ALBERT OF LOUVAIN

22

CECILIA

Martyr and patroness of music Third century

The earliest reference to this popular saint is in the fifth century *Sacramentary* by Pope Gelasius, though more historical evidence exists for her husband and brother-in-law. According to tradition, Cecilia was forced to marry a young Roman, Valerian, though she wanted to consecrate herself to God. Her reputation as patron of music probably originated with the story that she sang in her heart to God at her wedding. She converted Valerian by telling him that her virginity was protected by an angel he could only see if he was baptized. Valerian was executed before Cecilia for burying the bodies of martyrs, which was against the law. Cecilia won over 400 converts with her preaching before she was condemned. Her execution was botched, which gave her time to pray and preach to the crowds who had gone to see her die.

OTHER SAINTS • PHILEMON AND APPHIA

St Cecilia is known as the patroness of music.

The martyrdom of St Clement.

≈≈ 23 ≈≈

CLEMENT I
Pope and martyr d. 100?

This disciple of the Apostles was probably the third bishop of Rome after St Peter. He is traditionally associated with the Clement that St Paul mentions in Philippians as one of his fellow workers. A letter from Clement to the Corinthians is the earliest evidence of Rome's official intercession with a church outside its local authority. In the letter, Clement addresses a schism in the Corinthian church and exhorts them to follow the teachings of the Apostles. Legend says that the prefect of Rome exiled Clement to the marble quarries in Crimea after a riot against Christians in Rome. Clement ministered to other Christians at the quarries and converted pagans. For the latter crime, he was supposedly drowned in the sea by an anchor that was hung around his neck as he was flung over the side of a ship.

OTHER SAINTS • COLUMBANUS • GREGORY OF GIRGENTI • TROND

≈≈ 24 ≈≈

ANDREW DUNG LAC AND COMPANIONS
Martyrs of Vietnam Nineteenth century

Andrew, a native Vietnamese priest who was born in 1785 and died for the faith in 1839, is one of the 117 Vietnamese martyrs canonized by John Paul II. Christianity was introduced to Vietnam by French missionaries in the 17th century. The more successful the missionaries were in converting the Vietnamese, the more suspicious the rulers became. Persecution initially focused on the missionaries and native priests but eventually erupted in 60 years of purges in which as many as 300,000 Catholics suffered under Emperor Minh-Mang and Emperor Tu Duc in the 19th century. The group of martyrs includes 96 Vietnamese, 11 Spanish missionaries, and 10 French missionaries. Andrew was among the 50 priests killed at that time.

OTHER SAINTS • CHRYSOGONUS • COLMAN OF CLOYNE • ENFLEDA

✦ 25 ✦

MERCURIUS

Martyr d. 250?

The historical martyr Mercurius is described in legend as a Scythian soldier who served in Rome. The son of a Christian officer, Mercurius had neglected his faith. During a prolonged battle against barbarians, an angel appeared to Mercurius, told him not to forget the Lord, and gave him a sword that he used to kill the barbarian king. After the Emperor Decius promoted the new hero to general, Mercurius refused to sacrifice to the gods. Decius demanded an explanation for this apparent ingratitude. Mercurius said that Jesus had given him the victory, and he threw away the signs of his rank. He was then tortured and executed. Mercurius is venerated as one of the "warrior saints" in the East. In Egypt, he is called Abu Saifain, "the Father of Swords."

OTHER SAINTS ✦ MOSES OF ROME

✦ 26 ✦

JOHN BERCHMANS

Jesuit priest b. 1599, d. 1621

The eldest son of a Brabant shoemaker, John left school to help support his family. Intent on the priesthood, he became the servant of a cathedral priest so he could also study at the diocesan seminary. After he became a Jesuit novice, he walked from Antwerp to Rome to study at the Roman College. He distinguished himself not only in his studies, but also in his devotion and in acting out miracle plays. His spiritual practice was simple – to give great attention to little actions. He shunned excessive mortification saying that his penance was to live an ordinary life. After he had passed his examinations he fell ill. As his health deteriorated he maintained his cheerfulness and good humour, even asking a priest to say the after-meal grace when he'd swallowed some bitter medicine.

OTHER SAINTS ✦ PETER OF ALEXANDRIA ✦ SIRICIUS ✦ BASOLUS

✦ 27 ✦

JAMES INTERCISUS

Martyr d. 421

In 420, an overzealous bishop set fire to a pagan temple in Persia, igniting a retaliation against all Christians. James, a Christian serving in the Persian court, enjoyed power, wealth, and the favour of the king, Yazdigerd I. Fearful of losing everything, James stopped practicing his faith. When Yazdigerd died, however, James received a letter from his wife and his mother. Because of his cowardice, they had cut off communication with him until then. They reminded him that he had given up God's love for a king's favour. Where was that king now? they asked him. How could his dust grant James any more honours, let alone rescue him from hell? That letter acted like a mirror and James, horrified at the person he saw reflected in it, withdrew from the court,

"His name, Intercisus, means 'cut to pieces,' which was indeed the torment he had to endure to keep his soul intact."

giving up both his honours and wealth at the same time. When the new King, Bahram V, sent for him, James declared himself openly to be a Christian. The king immediately condemned James to have all of his limbs cut off one joint at a time. As the crowd gathered round to view the horrid spectacle, even the non-Christians begged James to reconsider his position. They encouraged him just to pretend to renounce his faith, so that he could avoid the torture. But James's days of using pretence to save his material life had been put firmly in the past. He reassured them that the death he was facing was a small price to pay for the eternal life he was going to. When the executioner cut off his thumb, the people again urged James to give up his riches instead of his body for the good of his soul, but James replied with Jesus' words, that whoever puts his hand to the plough and turns back isn't worthy of the kingdom of God. After all his limbs had been severed, he was beheaded. His name, Intercisus, means "cut to pieces," which was indeed the torment he had to endure to keep his soul intact.

OTHER SAINTS ✦ SECUNDINUS ✦ MAXIMUS OF RIEZ ✦ CONGAR

28

CATHERINE LABOURÉ

Nun and recipient of the Miraculous Medal b.1806, d.1876

Catherine could have been one of the most celebrated religious figures of her time, but instead she kept her reception of a popular religious message secret for 46 years. Four years after her mother's death, the 12-year-old Zoe (Catherine's birth name) took on the enormous responsibility of running the family household and raising her siblings. Despite opposition from her father and her lack of education, Zoe entered the Daughters of Charity when she was 24 years old, taking the religious name of Catherine. During her novitiate, she began to see visions of Mary, the mother of Jesus. In the second vision, Mary appeared with light streaming from her fingers. She was then replaced by a cross resting on a letter M, which in turn rested on two hearts

"For the rest of her life she served in a hospice for old men...

she said that she just couldn't help seeing Christ in them."

representing Jesus and Mary. Mary told Catherine she was to have a medal made to represent this vision, which symbolized Mary leading sinners to her son. Catherine's confessor, the only person Catherine told about the vision, refused to believe her for two years. The holiness of her character, prophecies that came to pass, and Catherine's general lack of imagination finally convinced him of her sincerity! He received permission to manufacture the medal. As millions of copies of what was later called the "Miraculous Medal" were distributed, Catherine remained insistent that no one know about the part she had played in its production. For the rest of her life she served in a hospice for old men, first in the kitchen, then the laundry, and finally taking charge of the care of the men. In this often tedious and thankless service she fed them, mended their clothes, organized recreation, nursed the sick, and comforted the dying – all with compassion. When other sisters accused her of being too kind to men who flouted her regulations, she said that she just couldn't help seeing Christ in them.

OTHER SAINTS • STEPHEN THE YOUNGER • SIMEON METAPHRASTE

Andrew was the first disciple of Jesus.

29

SATURNINUS OF TOULOUSE

Bishop and martyr d.257?

Saturninus was an African missionary sent to Gaul by Pope Fabian in 245. He settled in Toulouse where his preaching won many conversions – and the hostility of pagan priests. One day as he was walking home from his church, he passed the pagan temple and was dragged inside by the priests. They commanded him to sacrifice to the gods or else his own blood would be on the altar. Saturninus responded that the only sacrifice he would offer was one of praise to the true God. He warned his captors that their gods liked the sacrifices of their worshippers' souls more than that of animals. The priests tied his feet to the tail of a bull intended for sacrifice and goaded the bull to drag Saturninus around until he was dead.

OTHER SAINTS • FRANCIS OF LUCERA

30

ANDREW

Apostle First century

Andrew is known as the first disciple, the Protoclete or "first-called," because when John the Baptist said that Jesus was the Lamb of God, Andrew heard and went after Jesus. Andrew, a fisherman like his brother Simon Peter, came from the town of Bethsaida and lived with Peter's family in Capernaum. After talking to Jesus, Andrew was convinced that he was indeed the Messiah, and became the first evangelist, introducing Simon to Jesus. Later, he abandoned his boats and his livelihood to follow Jesus full-time, becoming one of the 12 Apostles. The earliest tradition reports that, after Pentecost, Andrew spread the Gospel to the Scythians, but other stories place him as far away as Russia. According to tradition, he was martyred by being tied to a cross shaped like an X – this cross is now known as St Andrew's cross.

OTHER SAINTS • CUTHBERT MAYNE • SAPOR AND ISAAC

1

ELIGIUS

Bishop and patron of metalworkers b.588?, d.660

Eligius was a master metalworker from Limoges who created exquisite shrines, vessels, and other ornaments. His scrupulous honesty led King Clothaire and his son Dagobert to trust him with responsible positions, such as master of the mint. Coins that Eligius minted bearing his name still exist. He was so generous to the needy that when someone asked for directions to Eligius's house they were told to look for the building with the crowd of poor people in front of it. Consecrated bishop of Noyon in 640, he dedicated himself to converting his people from superstitious and pagan beliefs. He especially condemned superstitious practices with a Christian appearance, such as wearing Scripture passages as charms.

OTHER SAINTS • ANSANUS THE BAPTIZER • AGERICUS OF VERDUN

2

JOHN RUYSBROECK

Mystic and writer b.1293, d.1381

One of the greatest mystical writers of all time was born in a small village near Brussels. When John was 11 years old he went to study in Brussels where he lived with an uncle who was a priest, John Heckaert. After John's ordination, his uncle formed a small contemplative community with his nephew and another priest, Francis van Coudenberg. In 1343, the three companions left Brussels for surroundings far from the distractions of the city. John wandered the forests of Soignes, listening to God, and writing his notes on wax tablets that were revised in his monastery cell. His works, especially *Spiritual Espousals*, promoted a fresh, practical approach to mysticism that, in combination with his reputation as spiritual director, made him known throughout Europe. He still remained humble, refusing to speak about himself to visitors.

OTHER SAINTS • VIVIAN • CHROMATIUS • EVASIUS OF BRESCIA

St Eligius worked with metals, to fashion beautiful objects.

3

FRANCIS XAVIER

Jesuit missionary and patron of foreign missions b.1506, d.1552

Francis Xavier was studying at the University of Paris for a lucrative clerical career when he got a new roommate, St Ignatius. Under his influence, Francis gave up his plans for a worldly life and joined Ignatius's small community, the beginning of the Jesuits. In 1540, Francis became the first Jesuit missionary outside of Europe. Throughout his travels in India, Indonesia, and Japan, Francis looked to his living books, as he called the people he met, to show him how to fit the Gospel message into their culture. Although he braved robbers, tigers, and disease, his greatest suffering came from loneliness. He wore signatures clipped from letters by his heart to keep him company. He died of a fever while trying to get into China, which was closed to foreigners.

OTHER SAINTS • LUCIUS • CASSIAN • MIROCLES OF MILAN • SOLA

4

JOHN DAMASCENE

Poet and Doctor of the Church b.690?, d.749?

One of the greatest poets of the church grew up as a Christian in Moslem-ruled Damascus. Far from being persecuted, his family was given trusted administrative positions at court. After being tutored by a monk who was liberated from slavery by John's father, John became chief official of revenue. He eventually followed his former tutor to the monastery of St Sabas where he wrote hymns and treatises promoting orthodox doctrine despite the disapproval of fellow monks who condemned his work as worldly distraction. Tradition says his abbot accused him of abandoning his vows, because John was singing instead of weeping. During the iconoclastic controversy, his strong defence of sacred images earned him the title "Doctor of Christian Art." His poetry has long been used in Catholic worship.

OTHER SAINTS • CLEMENT OF ALEXANDRIA • MARUTHAS

→ 5 →

SABAS
Hermit and abbot b.439, d.532

Sabas's uncles, who were supposed to care for him while his parents were away at battle, were more interested in who administered his parents' estate. Sabas ran away from their quarrelling and entered a monastery but eventually retreated to a cave that could only be accessed by rope. Though a monastery grew up around him, he continued to trek into the desert. Some monks, discontented at his absences, started their own community. When he heard that they were suffering, Sabas rescued them with land, food, and money. After he was put in charge of all the hermits in Palestine, Sabas took a more public role, using it to refute heresies. On one mission to the emperor, while other abbots asked for grants, Sabas requested only that he leave the church in peace.

OTHER SAINTS • CRISPINA • NICETIUS OF TRIER • SIGIRANUS

→ 6 →

NICHOLAS OF MYRA
Bishop Fourth century

This popular saint, who has evolved over the centuries into Santa Claus, was actually a bishop of Myra, but legends have obscured the few facts of his life. The tradition of Santa Claus bringing gifts at Christmas seems to have developed from the legend that Nicholas secretly threw bags of gold into a house to provide dowries for three impoverished girls. St Methodius credits Nicholas's preaching for Myra's complete rejection of the Arian heresy. Tradition relates that Nicholas carried this fervour for orthodoxy to the Nicean council where he was imprisoned for slapping the heretic Bishop Arius. A more forgiving Nicholas is shown in the stories that say he saved three condemned criminals by stopping an executioner's hand and later achieved clemency for accused officers by appearing to Constantine in a dream.

OTHER SAINTS • ASELLA OF ROME • ABRAHAM OF KRATIA

St Nicholas preached orthodoxy.

7

AMBROSE

Bishop, Doctor of the Church, and patron of learning b.339?, d.397

As governor of Milan, Ambrose was trying to calm a riot between Catholics and Arians when the crowd suddenly united in one thought – that Ambrose should be their new bishop. While bishop, he agreed to go on a diplomatic mission for the Arian Empress Justina to deter Maximus from invading Italy. But after Ambrose was successful, Justina turned on him and demanded that he surrender Milan's basilica to the Arians. Ambrose and his congregation barricaded themselves in the church. As Ambrose led them in hymns, the soldiers outside joined in, ending the siege peacefully. When Justina called on him again for help against Maximus, Ambrose not only agreed to negotiate, but warned her to flee when Maximus refused to retreat.

OTHER SAINTS • VICTOR OF PIACENZA • JOSEPHA ROSSELLO

8

ROMARIC

Abbot d.653

Romaric got an early lesson in the fickleness of worldly success when he lost his father and his inheritance during political upheavals in Merovingia. As the homeless boy knelt to beg a powerful bishop for help, the bishop kicked him in the face. His fortunes eventually turned, however, resulting in marriage, family, and an important office under King Clothaire II. Then a visiting monk, St Amatus, pointed out that Romaric was a slave to his possessions rather than their master. Romaric gave his property to the poor, freed his serfs, and became a monk at Luxeuil. The former noble became a talented gardener who memorized Psalms as he worked. Later, he and Amatus established a double monastery for men and women called Remiremont, where Romaric was joined by two of his daughters and two grandchildren.

9

JUAN DIEGO

Farmer, weaver, and recipient of the Vision of Our Lady of Guadalupe
b.1474, d.1548

Cuauhtlatoa, whose name means "eagle that speaks," was 27 years old when the Spanish conquered Tenochnitlán (now Mexico City). His Aztec culture was repressed and his religion forbidden. Not everyone could accept the faith of their conquerors willingly but Cuauhtlatoa's conversion was sincere. About 1524, he was baptized with his wife, taking the Christian name Juan Diego. A poor farmer and weaver, he walked 14 miles to Mexico City to receive religious instruction and to attend daily Mass before work. After his wife died in 1529, he went to live with his uncle Bernardino, without varying his devotion to his new faith. On December 9, 1531, he passed Tepayac hill as

"...as Juan let the roses spill from his cloak...a magnificent portrait

of the woman glowed on the inside of Juan's cloak."

usual on his way to Mass when his attention was arrested by music and light that didn't belong on the dusty road. Dressed like an Aztec princess with skin the same colour as Juan's, a beautiful woman appeared to tell him that she was the Virgin Mary. She had come to give the oppressed Mexicans her love and compassion. Despite Juan's protests that he was a nobody, she told him she wanted a church built on Tepayac. The bishop in Mexico City didn't believe this preposterous story from a poor Indian. So Juan returned with proof – roses Mary had given him in the middle of winter. But as Juan let the roses spill from his cloak, the bishop was transfixed by a different miracle – a magnificent portrait of the woman glowed on the inside of Juan's cloak. The church on Tepayac was dedicated to Mary under the name of Our Lady of Guadalupe. Juan Diego's cloak still exists and the image on it has remained as vibrant over the centuries as Mary's promise of love and compassion. Juan lived in a room near the chapel, devoting the rest of his life spreading Mary's message far and wide, like an eagle who could speak, just as his name suggests.

OTHER SAINTS • HIPPARCHUS AND COMPANIONS • LEOCADIA

10

EULALIA
Martyr d. 304?

This celebrated Spanish martyr reminds us to stand fast not just against great temptations but small compromises that may seem harmless. Eulalia was only 12 years old when Diocletian ordered the persecution of Christians. Eulalia's mother was terrified that her daughter's zeal would lead to her death and carried her away from the city. Eulalia ran away to confront the judge, Dacian, whom she accused of condemning souls by forcing them to sacrifice to idols. Dacian threatened her with torture, but promised that all she had to do to escape was simply touch the tip of her finger to a bit of incense. Eulalia recognized the trap in this seemingly small request and threw an idol to the floor as her answer. She was then tortured to death.

OTHER SAINTS · MILTIADES · GREGORY III

11

DAMASUS I
Pope d. 384

Damasus was a 60-year-old deacon when he was elected pope in 366. Though he faced hostile opposition throughout his papacy, Damasus conquered his opponents by initiating works that outlasted all of them. He commissioned Jerome to produce a new Latin translation of the Bible, known as the Vulgate, and changed the liturgical language of the church from Greek to Latin. He preserved and restored the catacombs and the graves and relics of the martyrs. In their honour he wrote epigrams, short paeans to their courage. The epigram he wrote about himself is carved on the empty papal crypt in the Roman cemetery. He says that he wished to be entombed there but was afraid he might offend the remains of the martyrs from the same cemetery. Damasus was buried elsewhere with his mother and sister.

OTHER SAINTS · VICTORICUS AND GENTIAN · DANIEL THE STYLITE

12

JANE FRANCES DE CHANTAL
Founder of the Visitation Order b. 1572, d. 1641

Despite early financial worries, Jane and her husband, Christophe, shared one heart and one soul and were devoted to their four children. Jane shared her blessings by feeding the poor who came to her door, even those who came back repeatedly, as she said that she hoped God would never turn her away when she kept making the same request. Her happy life ended when her husband was killed in a hunting accident and she went to care for her elderly father-in-law, who rewarded her with insults and abuse. This suffering led her to a deep spiritual life and to St Francis de Sales, her director and best friend. Jane's Visitation Order welcomed women rejected by other orders because of poor health or age, in order to give everyone a chance to follow their calling.

OTHER SAINTS · FINIAN OF CLONARD · CORENTIN · VICELIN

13

LUCY
Martyr and patroness of sufferers of eye disease d. 304

Though this martyr's name means "light," her life is shrouded in mystery. It seems that a young woman from Syracuse, named Lucy, died for her faith in the early fourth century. According to legend, her mother arranged her marriage to a pagan despite Lucy's vow to devote her life to Christ. But when her chronically ill mother regained health as a result of Lucy's prayers, Lucy was given permission to follow her heart. The rejected bridegroom, however, betrayed Lucy by revealing that she was a Christian. The governor sentenced her to a brothel but the guards couldn't move her to take her there. She was tortured and finally killed. Because Lucy's eyes were supposedly put out and then restored by a miracle, she is often depicted carrying a dish with her eyes and is invoked as patroness of those with eye problems.

OTHER SAINTS · JUDOC · AUTBERT · ODILIA

St Lucy's torture involved having her eyes taken out but God restored them — she is now known as patroness of those with eye diseases.

14

JOHN OF THE CROSS
Mystic and Doctor of the Church b.1542, d.1591

This contemplative monk was considered such a danger by his fellow Carmelites that they kidnapped and imprisoned him. John had joined St Teresa of Avila's reformed Carmelite Order and drawn the hostility of those who opposed her ideas. In the darkness of his cell, John forged the mystical union with God that he later expressed in timeless works including *Ascent of Mount Carmel* and *Dark Night of the Soul.* John eventually engineered an escape because he missed being able to celebrate Mass. He hid out in convents where he shared what he had learned as well as the mystical poetry he had composed. John never did escape the resentment directed against him and died alone, humiliated but still burning with the love of God.

OTHER SAINTS • SPIRIDION • NICASIUS • VENANTIUS FORTUNATUS

15

MARY PAULA DI ROSA
Founder of the Servants of Charity b.1813, d.1885

When soldiers intent on plunder pounded on the hospital door in Brescia, they were blocked by a frail sister holding a great crucifix. Shamefully, the erstwhile raiders slunk into the shadows unaware that Paula faced all her challenges just as fearlessly. She once said that she could never sleep with a clear conscience if she had missed a chance to do some good. Starting with parish retreats and a women's guild she organized at 17 years of age, she moved on to supervise a workhouse for girls at the age of 24. When no one would provide a safe place for the girls to stay, she quit and established a boarding house. Appointed superior of the newly founded Servants of Charity at 27 years of age, she won respect for her nuns in hospitals that had previously seen religious nurses as an intrusion in their secular world.

OTHER SAINTS • VALERIAN AND COMPANIONS • PAUL OF LATROS

16

ADELAIDE
Empress b.931, d.999

Adelaide's stormy life provided many tests for her forgiving nature. Her husband, King of Italy, was reportedly poisoned by his successor Berengarius. When Adelaide refused to marry the usurper's son, he had her beaten and imprisoned. She was able to escape through a hole in the wall and took refuge with a relative who called on Otto, the King of Germany and future emperor, for help. Otto married her and they had five children. After Otto's death, her own son, Otto II, and her daughter-in-law forced her into exile because of her political influence with their subjects. She remained generous and peace-loving, and became regent for her grandson after her son's death. She died on a mission to Burgundy to reconcile the king, her nephew, with his subjects.

17

STURMI
Abbot d.779

Sturmi suffered not only from his opponents, but from those who tried to help him. After ordination, Sturmi emulated his mentor, St Boniface, by evangelizing Westphalia. When Sturmi wanted to establish a monastery, Boniface's vague directions to a possible location led him on a frightening quest before he found Fulda. The pope granted Sturmi privileges that were resented by Boniface's successor, Lull, who had him banished. Sturmi's monks rose in protest and got King Pepin to reinstate their founder. But the support of Emperor Charlemagne caused lasting damage to Sturmi's work. He had treated the Saxons so brutally that they hated his faith and drove Sturmi away as soon as he left. Sturmi returned after the revolt was suppressed, but died soon after from an accidental overdose of medication given by a doctor.

OTHER SAINTS • LAZARUS • OLYMPIAS • BEGGA • WIVINA

St Adelaide was always generous, despite her own troubles.

18

WINEBALD
Abbot d. 761

When Winebald fell ill on a pilgrimage to the Holy Land, he watched his brother St Willibald continue without him. Forced to remain in Rome, he began to study and grew to love the city. While visiting, St Boniface convinced him to join the evangelization of Germany. There, far from his native England and the place where they parted, Winebald was reunited with his brother, now bishop of Eichstadt. Willibald put Winebald and their sister St Walburga in charge of the double monastery, Heidenheim. Winebald reminded his monks that the best evangelization was the example of their lives modelled on Christ. Despite chronic illness, he attempted to continue his missionary travels and died in the arms of his brother and sister.

OTHER SAINTS • GATIAN OF TOURS • BODAGISIL • FLANNAN

19

URBAN V
Pope b. 1309, d. 1370

A distinguished professor of canon law, this pope asserted that ignorance was the first sin of Christians and worked to rectify that situation by establishing universities and scholarships. He had also used his diplomatic skills before being elected pope by bringing about an alliance with Emperor Charles IV and making overtures of reunion with the Eastern Church. The papacy had been in exile in Avignon, France, for 50 years, but when he became pope, Urban courageously returned to Rome despite the objections of the French court and the cardinals. Unfortunately, attacks on Rome forced him to return to Avignon, where he died four months later. Never forgetting his Benedictine vows, he abhorred pomp and luxury and had himself moved to his brother's house in his last days, so that he could die in plain surroundings.

OTHER SAINTS • NEMESIUS AND COMPANIONS • ANASTASIUS I

20

DOMINIC OF SILOS
Abbot d. 1073

After entering the monastery of San Millán de la Cogolla, this former peasant became novice master and then prior. When the King of Navarre confiscated the monastery's estates, Dominic was forced to flee to Old Castile where he was appointed abbot of the monastery of St Sebastian of Silos. The dilapidated, bankrupt monastery was no prize but under Dominic it became the most famous monastery in Spain. He restored it in Romanesque style and created a metal workshop to support the monastery and poor of the area. A lover of illuminated manuscripts, he established a scriptorium that produced volumes of literary treasures. He transformed the monastery into a learning centre and preserved the ancient Mozarbic liturgy and Visigothic script.

OTHER SAINTS • AMMON AND COMPANIONS • PHILOGONIUS

21

PETER CANISIUS
Jesuit priest and Doctor of the Church b. 1521, d. 1597

The Jesuit who would be known as the Second Apostle of Germany was a native of the Netherlands. Through his writings, preaching, and reforms he brought about a renewal of the Catholic faith in his adopted land. After serving as a delegate to the Council of Trent, Peter was given the difficult charge of counteracting unorthodox teaching at the university at Ingolstadt. He was so successful that he was sent to Vienna, which was in such bad shape that no priest had been ordained there for two decades. Suspicion of this foreign priest changed to trust when the Viennese witnessed his dedicated ministrations during a plague. Though Peter agreed to administer the diocese, he turned down the bishopric. He also argued so forcefully for a catechism that he was ordered to write it himself. Though Peter considered himself a poor writer, he reasoned that that was no excuse to keep silent. His catechism was an immediate success, appearing in more than 200 editions in his lifetime, and he went on to write treatises and volumes that earned him the title of Doctor of the Church. As Jesuit provincial of southern Germany and Austria, he established colleges so respected that even Protestants attended them. But Peter's work wasn't confined to lecture halls or writing desks. In 1565, he smuggled the decrees of the Council of Trent past brigands and hostile Protestants to the European bishops. Though energetic in promoting his faith, he believed the power of patience and compassion would succeed where violence would fail. When a brilliant but emotionally ill priest, Couvillon, alienated his companions and students, Peter wouldn't let him resign and appointed him as his secretary. He then used work, responsibility, and prayer to direct Couvillon's thoughts away from himself towards successful service.

OTHER SAINTS • SEVERINUS OF TRÈVES • JOHN VINCENT

22

FRANCES XAVIER CABRINI
Founder of the Missionary Sisters of the Sacred Heart b.1850, d.1917

The first US citizen to be canonized arrived in New York City as an Italian immigrant sent to serve other immigrants. Discrimination against Italians made it difficult to get permission or funds to support her work but she refused to give up. She established or took over 67 institutions including hospitals, schools, and orphanages in Europe and North and South America. To get to those in need, Frances climbed the Andes, descended into mines, walked the slums of New Orleans, and explored the Panama jungles. She did whatever she could, teaching children, visiting benefactors, sewing clothes for students, and even carrying bricks to build a hospital. Once a bishop asked a woman sweeping the hall to let Mother Cabrini know he had arrived. The servant returned in more appropriate dress to introduce herself – as Frances Cabrini.

OTHER SAINTS • ZENO OF NICOMEDIA • CHAEREMON • ISCHYRION

Dominic enthroned as the abbot of Silos.

23

JOHN OF KANTY

Priest b.1390?, d.1473

At the age of 41, John was forced from the University of Cracow by rivals who engineered false charges against the popular professor. Banished to Olkusz as apprentice pastor, he faced further hostility from parishioners who knew he was in disgrace. By the time he was exonerated, his parishioners had grown to love him so much that they followed him down the road back to Cracow. For the rest of his life, John taught Scripture and his philosophy that faith should be defended with humour and kindness, not with harshness that endangered the debater's soul and cause. John's own compassion was evident in his concern for the needs of others. Once, at dinner, he jumped up with his plate in his hand, and ran to give his food to a beggar he had seen walking by.

OTHER SAINTS • MARTYRS OF CRETE • VICTORIA AND ANATOLIA

24

CHARBEL MAKLOUF

Hermit b.1828, d.1898

In the mountains of Lebanon Charbel was raised by an uncle who didn't appreciate the young boy's love of prayer and solitude, so Charbel joined the Lebanese Maronite Order secretly at 23 years of age. During his novitiate he was discouraged by monks who doubted his vocation and relatives who wanted him to go back home, but his determination led to profession and ordination. After 16 years at a monastery at Annaya, he received permission to live as a hermit about a mile from the monastery in imitation of the early desert hermits. His austere life was spent speaking only when required, eating the plainest food, sleeping with a wooden pillow, and putting himself under the obedience of anyone sharing the hermitage. He died following a stroke he suffered while celebrating the Eucharist.

OTHER SAINTS • GREGORY OF SPOLETO • IRMINA AND ADELA

25

JACOPONE OF TODI

Lay brother b.1230?, d.1306

Jacomo was a lawyer in Umbria when his wife was killed after only a year of marriage. Grief drove him to devote himself to public penance so eccentric, such as wearing a bridle and saddle, that the town nicknamed him Jacopone, after a legendary fool. He finally found stability by joining the Franciscans as a lay brother and began to produce mystical and religious poetry that became popular. During a controversy over Franciscan practice, he supported the losing side, even against the pope. His outspoken criticism led to his imprisonment for five years. He repented and spent the time in penance, writing poetry. He was released after the death of the pope and spent his last years in peace. He is credited with the hymn "Stabat Mater Dolorosa."

OTHER SAINTS • EUGENIA • ANASTASIA

26

STEPHEN

Protomartyr and deacon d.35?

The first problem that the young Christian community faced after Pentecost was one of practical charity and accusations of discrimination. The members of Hellenistic Jewish background complained that their widows were being neglected in favour of those of Palestinian Jewish heritage. The Apostles recognized the problem as a broader one, requiring a thoughtful solution. They didn't have enough time to both preach the Gospel and care for the needs of the community so they commissioned seven disciples by the laying on of hands to serve the community as deacons. The first of these was Stephen, whose Greek name showed he would be a choice approved by the Hellenistic party. But Stephen also had other qualifications, particularly the fact that he was filled with faith and the Holy Spirit. It was the Holy Spirit

John the Evangelist survived being burned in oil.

that drove Stephen to continue preaching about Jesus in the streets, and perform great miracles in Jesus' name. Some Jews from Asia tried to win debates over him and, when they failed, manufactured charges of blasphemy against him and brought him before the Jewish council of the Sanhedrin. At first, Stephen's appearance made it difficult to believe the charges because he had the face of an angel. When the high priest asked Stephen if the charges were correct, Stephen answered with a sermon explaining how Jesus was the Messiah foretold in Hebrew Scripture. He ended by saying their ancestors were guilty of persecuting the prophets as well as ignoring the law. Then he looked up to heaven and announced that he saw Jesus standing at the right hand of God. He was immediately dragged out of town and stoned to death. Stephen's last words were a prayer of forgiveness for his murderers, asking God not to hold the sin against them. Stephen is known as the protomartyr because he was the first martyr of the Christian community.

OTHER SAINTS • ARCHELAUS • ZOSIMUS • TATHAI OF WALES

JOHN THE EVANGELIST
Apostle d. 100?

John was a Galilean fisherman who, with his brother James, was called by Jesus to follow him. John was close to Jesus, witnessing his transfiguration, laying his head on his chest at the last supper, and accompanying him to Gethsemane. The only Apostle present at Jesus' crucifixion, he was charged with the care of Jesus' mother Mary. After Pentecost, tradition says that he went to Ephesus. During Domitian's persecution, he was condemned to be boiled in oil but survived miraculously and was banished to the island of Patmos, where he recorded his revelations. After Domitian's death, he returned to Ephesus to write his mystical Gospel and three Epistles. When he grew too weak with age to preach, he simply repeated the command to love one another over and over, saying that if people only did that, it would be enough.

OTHER SAINTS • FABIOLA • NICARETE

28

ANTONY OF LÉRINS
Hermit d.520?

Born near the contemporary borders of Austria, Hungary, and Croatia, Antony found refuge from barbarian invasions, and the grief of losing his father, in the care of St Severinus. After St Severinus's death in 482, Antony went to live with an uncle, a bishop in Bavaria. But monastery life didn't provide enough peace for him and he left for Italy six years later. There he studied under the hermit St Marius on Lake Como before retiring to the opposite side of the lake, where he lived in a cave, prayed, and tended his garden. A story is told that he discerned that one of his disciples was in fact a murderer fleeing justice. This tale and others brought too much attention to Antony and he travelled over the Alps to spend the rest of his days in Lérins.

OTHER SAINTS • HOLY INNOCENTS • CAESARIUS OF ARMENIA

29

THOMAS BECKET
Archbishop of Canterbury and martyr b.1118, d.1170

Thomas's political successes as archdeacon of Canterbury and his engaging personality won him the friendship of Henry II and the position of chancellor. Although he fulfilled his duties, he lived magnificently and was accused of forgetting his clerical orders when he engaged in armed combat. When King Henry proposed electing him archbishop of Canterbury, Thomas warned him it would end their friendship, a prediction that came true. Thomas adopted an austere lifestyle and a determined stance in defence of church rights. Henry's frustration with Thomas led to persecution, and he even complained that no one would rid him of this meddling priest. Four knights interpreted this as permission for murder and killed Thomas as he entered the church for vespers. Henry II did public penance for his responsibility in Thomas's death.

OTHER SAINTS • TROPHIMUS OF ARLES • MARCELLUS AKIMETES

30

ANYSIA OF THESSALONICA
Martyr d.304

Anysia was a rich young Christian woman who, having decided to consecrate her life to the Lord, followed his commandment and sold her possessions to give the money to the poor. Despite the law against Christian assemblies, she continued to attend worship. One day she was stopped by a guard who demanded to know where she was going. Startled by his appearance, she made the sign of the cross on her forehead. When he demanded her identity and destination again, she replied that she was a servant of Christ on the way to worship. He grabbed hold of her, threatening to take her to sacrifice to the gods instead. When she struggled, he ran her through with his sword. Anysia is an example to anyone who takes the right to worship for granted.

OTHER SAINTS • SABINUS AND COMPANIONS • ANYSIUS

31

MELANIA THE YOUNGER
Mother and helper of the poor b.393?, d.439

Though this granddaughter of St Melania the Elder wanted to consecrate her life to God, her father forced her to marry because of her rank and wealth. When she almost died in childbirth, her husband, Pinian, vowed that if she recovered he would let her do as she wished. He kept his promise, and accompanied Melania and her mother to a villa that they converted into a hospice and convent. Melania sold her estates to help the poor and reportedly freed 8000 slaves within two years. To escape the Goths, Melanian, Pinian, and her mother fled to Africa, where St Augustine honoured Melania and Pinian as true lights of the church. The three moved on to a contemplative life in Jerusalem where her mother and husband died and Melania established a convent near their graves.

OTHER SAINTS • SYLVESTER I • COLUMBA OF SENS

Thomas Becket (right) always stood up for the church, even when it meant he had to disagree with his old friend the king.

S. THOMAS   S. MARTINVS

INDEX

PICTURE CREDITS

Acknowledgements in Page Order

1 The Art Archive; 2 Bridgeman Art Library/Musee Conde; 3 AKG, London; 4 Bridgeman Art Library; 5 Bridgeman Art Library; 6 Sonia Halliday Photographs; 7 Bridgeman Art Library/Phillips; 8 Bridgeman Art Library; 9 Sotheby's Picture Library; 10 The Art Archive; 11 AKG, London; 12 Bridgeman Art Library; 17 Gene Plaisted; 19 AKG, London; 20 Bridgeman Art Library; 22 Bridgeman Art Library; 24 The Art Archive; 27 Bridgeman Art Library; 28 Bridgeman Art Library/Francesco Turio Bohm; 30 Bridgeman Art Library; 33 The Art Archive; 34 Gene Plaisted; 37 Scala; 38 Bridgeman Art Library; 41 Scala/Vatican Archives; 42 Sonia Halliday Photographs; 45 The Art Archive; 47 Scala; 48 AKG, London; 51 AKG, London; 52 AKG, London/British Library; 54 Bridgeman Art Library; 57 Bridgeman Art Library; 58 Sotheby's Picture Library; 60 The Art Archive/Civic Museum, Rimini; 63 Gene Plaisted; 65 Gene Plaisted; 67 Sonia Halliday Photographs; 68 Sotheby's Picture Library; 71 Bridgeman Art Library; 72 Sonia Halliday Photographs; 75 York Minster; 77 Bridgeman Art Library; 78 Bridgeman Art Library/Toledo Museum; 81 Bridgeman Art Library; 82 Bridgeman Art Library/Louvre, Paris; 85 AKG, London; 87 Bridgeman Art Library; 88 Bridgeman Art Library; 90 AKG, London; 93 Bridgeman Art Library/Museo Correr, Venice; 94 Gene Plaisted; 96 AKG, London/Cameraphoto; 99 Bridgeman Art Library/Caylus Anticuario, Madrid; 101 Bridgeman Art Library; 102 The Art Archive; 105 The Art Archive; 106 The Art Archive; 108 The Art Archive; 110 Scala; 113 Bridgeman Art Library; 114 AKG, London/Tretyakov Gallery, Moscow; 117 AKG, London/Erich Lessing; 118 Gene Plaisted; 121 AKG, London/Cameraphoto; 122 Bridgeman Art Library/Private Collection; 125 AKG, London/Museo Del Prado; 126 The Art Archive/Saragozza Museum; 129 AKG, London; 131 AKG, London; 132 Sonia Halliday Photographs; 134 Sonia Halliday Photographs; 136 AKG, London/Galleria dell Academia, Venice; 138 Bridgeman Art Library; 140 AKG, London/Cameraphoto; 143 Bridgeman Art Library; 145 AKG, London/S, Domingie; 147 Bridgeman Art Library/Private Collection; 148 Bridgeman Art Library; 151 AKG, London; 152 York Minster; 154 Bridgeman Art Library; 156 AKG, London; 159 Bridgeman Art Library; 160 Bridgeman Art Library; 162 Scala; 164 AKG, London; 167 Sonia Halliday Photographs/Sonia Halliday and Laura Lushington; 169 AKG, London; 171 AKG, London/Museo Del Prado; 172 Bridgeman Art Library/York City Art Gallery; 174 The Art Archive; 176 Bridgeman Art Library; 178 AKG, London/Munchen Kunsthandel; 181 Bridgeman Art Library; 182 Sonia Halliday Photographs/Sonia Halliday and Laura Lushington; 185 Bridgeman Art Library; 187 Bridgeman Art Library/Christie's Images, London; 189 Bridgeman Art Library/Palazzo Ducale, Urbino.